China, Japan, and Senkaku Islands

Conflict in the East China Sea Amid an American Shadow

Other Books Authored by Monika Chansoria

Nuclear China: A Veiled Secret (2014)

China: Military Modernisation and Strategy (2011)

Chinese WMD Proliferation in Asia: US Response (2009)

Edited Volume

Pakistan's Tactical Nuclear Weapons: Conflict Redux (co-edited, 2014)

China, Japan, and Senkaku Islands

Conflict in the East China Sea Amid an American Shadow

Dr Monika Chansoria

KNOWLEDGE WORLD
KW Publishers Pvt Ltd
New Delhi

in association with

Centre for Land Warfare Studies
New Delhi

The Centre for Land Warfare Studies (CLAWS), New Delhi, is an autonomous think tank dealing with contemporary issues of national security and conceptual aspects of land warfare, including conventional and sub-conventional conflicts and terrorism. CLAWS conducts research that is futuristic in outlook and policy-oriented in approach.

Centre for Land Warfare Studies
RPSO Complex, Parade Road, Delhi Cantt, New Delhi 110010
Tel: +91.11.25691308 Fax: +91.11.25692347
Email: landwarfare@gmail.com Website: www.claws.in

ISBN 978-93-83649-99-0

Published in India by
Kalpana Shukla
KW Publishers Pvt Ltd
4676/21, First Floor, Ansari Road, Daryaganj, New Delhi 110002
Tel: +91.11.23263498 / 43528107 Email: knowledgeworld@kwpub.com
Website: www.kwpub.com

2011 FIPBA BEST PUBLISHERS AWARD (ENGLISH)

Printed and bound by Gopsons.

CONTENTS

Fondly, for my loving parents

|| अनुगृहितोऽस्मि ||

FOREWORD

The East China Sea is central to the power dynamics in the wider Indo-Pacific region, now the global hub of maritime security challenges. Monika Chansoria's book highlights the importance of the East China Sea as a new centre of geo-political gravity by focussing on the strategic dimensions of the dispute triggered by China's increasingly assertive claim to the Japanese-controlled Senkaku Islands. The dispute is integral to China's larger ambition to fashion a Sino-centric Asia by challenging Japan in the East China Sea and India in the Indian Ocean and by asserting control to most of the South China Sea. In fact, as part of its quest for supremacy at sea, China has sought to extend its maritime frontiers by creating artificial islands and claiming sovereignty over them and their surrounding waters in the South China Sea and by declaring an Air Defence Identification Zone (ADIZ) in the East China Sea that extends to islands that it covets but does not control.

In this light, the East China Sea is critical to the contest for influence in the Indo-Pacific region, where the proliferation of submarines is already underscoring an undersea arms race. More than half of the world's submarines are likely to operate in the Indo-Pacific region. As China rapidly expands its submarine fleet, its actions and assertiveness are prompting other countries to step up their naval modernisation. Determined to take the sea route to secure global power status and to challenge the US-led international order, China is stepping up its strategic role and presence in the East and South China Seas in particular.

The East China Sea, against this background, is important not just for China and Japan but also for the outside powers – from India and Australia to the United States and South Korea —because what happens there will impinge on the power equilibrium in the Asia-Pacific and on the international maritime order. China's consolidation of power in the East China Sea will also have a direct bearing on the maritime and security interests of the extra-regional players. In fact, developments in the East China Sea carry the potential of upending even the current liberal world order, if brute power were to trump rules. The dispute over the Senkakus, as this book brings out, is, thus, more than just a bilateral matter between Japan and China.

China's elevation of its claim to the Senkakus to a "core interest" has made the prospect of resolving the dispute more difficult. Beijing has not only hardened its claim to the Senkakus but also some in China have gone to the extent of questioning Japan's sovereignty over even Okinawa. Furthermore, with increasing frequency, China has dispatched ships and warplanes into Japan's territory around the tiny Senkakus. All this suggests that China has little interest in ending the dispute any time soon or settling it peacefully.

However, unlike in the South China Sea – where Beijing has continued its territorial creep and trashed an international arbitral tribunal's ruling that held that it has no legal or historical basis to claim most of the region – China has found the going tough in the East China Sea.

China's leaders may have thought that undertaking aggressive activities such as the increasing intrusions into Japan's air space and territorial waters, and even dangerous actions that could cause a contingency situation, would compel Tokyo to bow to their demands. Instead, their actions have accomplished the opposite—shaken Japan out of its complacency and diffidence and set in motion Japan's political resurrection. Japan is beefing up its military capabilities to defend the Senkakus and some 400 other islands that serve as markers for its territorial waters. Japan has also strengthened its alliance with the US and forged new strategic ties with India and some other Asian states. The Japanese government, by easing a longstanding, self-imposed ban on arms exports, boosting defence spending, and asserting its right to exercise "collective self-defence," has opened the path for Japan to collaborate more actively with friendly states.

China's territorial assertiveness, by contributing to Japanese insecurity, is also fostering conditions for constitutional reform in Japan. No other country in the world is bound by the kind of constitutional restrictions that were imposed on a vanquished Japan by the occupying American forces after World War II.

Yet Japan has clung to its US-imposed Constitution without so much as carrying out a single amendment, even as the United States has enacted six amendments to its own Constitution in this period. Today, US security interests would be better served by a more confident and secure Japan that assumes greater responsibility for its own defence and for East Asian security. Japan is the only power that can block China from gaining ascendancy in the region. If the US lends open support to constitutional reform in Japan, it will not only blunt Chinese criticism of the move but also assuage the concerns of many Japanese who link the Constitution with the long period of peace the country has enjoyed.

This book highlights why peace in Asia demands a proactive Japan. Japan is not turning its back on pacifism but improving its defence capabilities to repulse aggression and to proactively contribute to peace. Tokyo recognises that national-security reforms that enable Japan to defend itself better, including by building mutually beneficial regional partnerships, would enhance Japanese capacity to forestall the emergence of a destabilising power imbalance in East Asia and the wider Indo-Pacific region.

More broadly, the East China Sea's centrality to the wider geo-politics, balance of power, and maritime order should induce like-minded states to work closely together to positively shape developments there, including by ensuring that unilateralism is not cost-free.

As this very timely and valuable study underscores, the rest of the world has much at stake in the Japan-China dispute over the Senkakus. Attempts to disturb the territorial status quo and peace in East Asia would likely create a systemic risk to stability and prosperity in the Asia-Pacific region.

BRAHMA CHELLANEY
Professor
Centre for Policy Research, New Delhi

Preface

Conventional arguments alone cannot fully seize the dualistic and complex nature of the Senkaku Islands and the ostensible dispute advocated by China that engulfs them. There are several intertwined compulsions, motivations, and legalities that have driven, and shall continue driving the debate. Territorial disputes are best approached eclectically, through a viable structured framework, given that it studies the impact of military technological growth on willingness and opportunity, a conception of contiguity that reflects maritime territory, and the impact of regime types on state willingness to pursue military means of conflict resolution. States which are more likely to adopt aggressive, military-oriented foreign policy practices when faced with real or perceived threats to territory, are put through the litmus test of the web of economic symbiosis – as amply demonstrated in the case of the Senkaku Islands.

While the mission of the Chinese armed forces stretches beyond the nation's maritime and land territories, present-day China is said to be "adjusting to keep up with the pace of its rise". This clearly spells out the dichotomy in Beijing's interpretation and application of power, both militarily and politically. As much as China bawls for what it describes as "peaceful rise/development", coupled with incessant banality that Beijing shall "never seek hegemony", its constant attempts to create fresh status quo in almost all its existing territorial disputes, including Chinese frigates sailing for the first time through the "contiguous zone" near the Senkaku Islands this summer, make the writing on the wall quite clear. Beijing, progressively, is attempting to burnish a no-compromise stance on territorial issues, in both the East China and South China Seas.

Effective employment of application of power determinants in the political, diplomatic and military realms to promote overall influence in its periphery has assumed verve in China's long-term strategic foreign policy agenda. A militarily expansionist China is seemingly biding its time until its force modernisation stands complete – with a substantial share of reforms likely to begin yielding results from 2020 onwards. What is most critical in here is the timing. The year 2021 establishes 100 years since the founding of the Chinese Communist Party and 2049 shall usher in 100 years of the People's Republic of China coming into existence as a nation-state. Realisation of these twin bicentennial goals remains the nucleus of Xi Jinping's "China Dream", most significantly including the vital goal of national rejuvenation (essentially meant to be read as reunification).

The core assumption of liberal international theories positing that interdependence (more specifically, economic symbiosis) among states influences state behaviour, remains much in divergence to the realist paradigm. While economic interaction appears to be the ideal driver for states to adopt cooperative frameworks, the pressing geo-strategic realities and objectives have perennially been the pivot that holds the potential to invade any/all regional realignments. The trajectory of China's present equations with key Asian players is a testament to this submission.

Asia's bitter historical legacies have indelibly blotched the geo-political future, triggering an acute security dilemma between China and Japan, which undeniably shall have profound ramifications for East Asia. In the backdrop of the East China Sea's brewing dispute, my book traces the genesis of the Senkaku Islands, their history, and potential future, and chronicles the voyage of Sino-Japanese relations, by virtue of multiple prisms, in the explicit context of the Senkaku Islands.

New Delhi **Dr Monika Chansoria**
August 2016

1. The Genesis of Dispute in the East China Sea

Conflict in East Asia is seemingly trapped in an unending state, that of perpetuity of a geo-strategic struggle, with ties between China and Japan getting increasingly strained over the very bitterly contested territorial row involving the Senkaku Gunto (Islands) which China terms as the Diaoyu Islands (meaning "fishing platform"). The dispute over sovereignty of the Senkaku/Diaoyu Islands is structured around economic interests, domestic political compulsions, issues surrounding national identity and allegiance, requirements of international law and the long-standing baggage of historical grievances. The eight uninhabited islands that comprise the Senkakus are a sum of five small volcanic islands and three rocky outcroppings, with a total land area of 6.32 sq km, scattered in the geographical location of 25.8333° N, 123.5833° E (North Latitude/East Longitude).[1] Senkaku Islands is more of a collective term referring to a group of islands which include Uotsuri, Kitakojima, Minamikojima, Kuba, Taisho, Okinokitaiwa, Okinominamiiwa, and Tobise located on the west side of Japan's Nansei-shotō Islands – a chain of volcanic Japanese islands stretching southwest from Kyushu to Taiwan: the Ōsumi, Tokara, Amami, Okinawa, and Sakishima Islands (further divided into the Miyako and Yaeyama Islands). The largest of these is Okinawa, part of Ishigaki city, Okinawa prefecture. The Senkaku Islands are located in the East China Sea, northeast of Taiwan, east of the Chinese mainland and southwest of Japan's southernmost Okinawa prefecture. In terms of distance, they are situated approximately 170 km north of Ishigaki Island, 380 km from Wenzhou on the Chinese mainland and 180 km northeast of Keelung, Taiwan.

Fig 1.1: Map of Senkaku (Diaoyu) Islands and the Surrounding Region

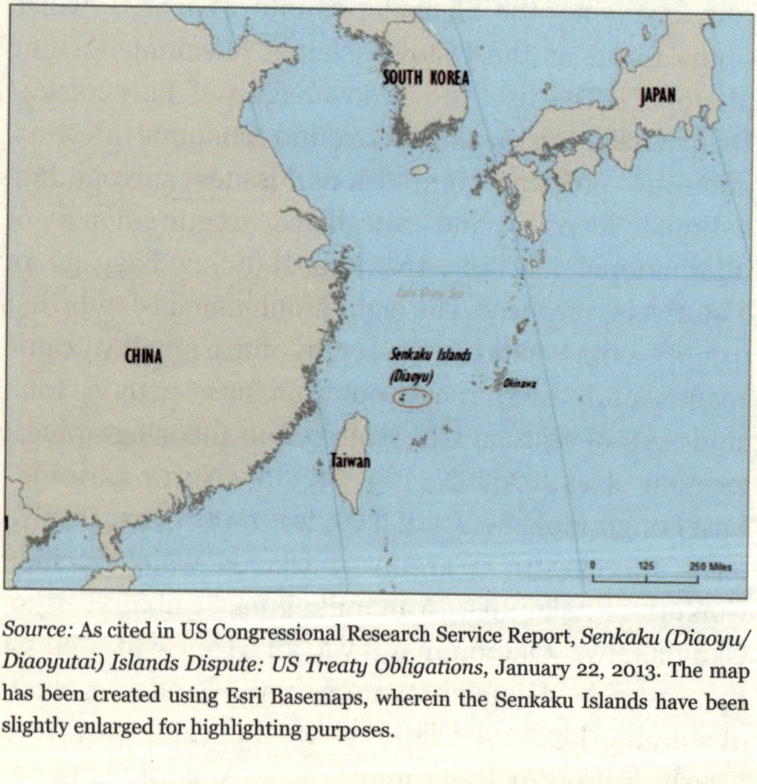

Source: As cited in US Congressional Research Service Report, *Senkaku (Diaoyu/Diaoyutai) Islands Dispute: US Treaty Obligations*, January 22, 2013. The map has been created using Esri Basemaps, wherein the Senkaku Islands have been slightly enlarged for highlighting purposes.

Treaty of Shimonoseki and the Japanese Claim

The historical past of this dispute is complex and needs to be segmented in significant sections in order to understand the key milestones which define the course of the chronicled journey of the Senkaku Islands. Recalling history, World War II broke out in Asia with the second Sino-Japanese War of 1937 and the eventual halt of the Japanese campaign brought about by the United States in 1945. Prior to that, the Cairo Declaration was adopted in 1943 by the US, UK and Chiang Kai-shek. The declaration developed ideas from the 1941 Atlantic Charter, which was issued by the Allied powers of World War II to set goals for the post-war order. The Cairo Communiqué was broadcast through radio on December 01, 1943. The Cairo Declaration is cited in Clause Eight (8) of the Potsdam Declaration – referred to by the Japanese Instrument of Surrender.

The declaration stated that Japan shall return all territories it had seized or occupied from China such as Manchuria, Formosa and the Pescadores. Following defeat in the first Sino-Japanese War, which broke out in August 1894, China signed the Treaty of Shimonoseki (Shimonoseki Jōyaku) on April 17, 1895, as part of which, apart from having to pay a large indemnity, there was agreement between the Empire of Japan and the Chinese Qing Empire (1644-1912), that China shall cede the Pescadores Islands, the Liaodong Peninsula, all islands appertaining to Taiwan and the island of Taiwan itself. Notably, the Treaty of Shimonoseki was not only a treaty of peace but also a treaty of cession, which ended the first Sino-Japanese War. Following the Treaty of Shimonoseki, there was sufficient evidence that Japan exercised effective control over the Senkaku Islands, including a significant lease of the islands to a Japanese citizen since 1896. While the Shimonoseki Treaty included ceding of Taiwan and the Pescadores, it, however, did not mention the Senkaku Islands. In fact, the islands were not even discussed during the negotiating sessions, with Article 2 of the treaty stating:[2]

> China cedes to Japan in perpetuity and full sovereignty, the following territories, together with all fortifications, arsenals, and public property thereon...(b) The island of Formosa, together with *all islands appertaining or belonging* to the said island of Formosa [emphasis added].

Ten years after the first Sino-Japanese War, Japan defeated Russia and took control of the industrial base in Manchuria (northeast China) in 1905. Five years later, Japan invaded Korea in 1910 and established it as a Japanese colony.[3]

In contrast to many other occupied islands, the Senkaku/Diaoyu Islands were not explicitly mentioned even in the Cairo Declaration of 1943, when it declared "... Japan shall be stripped of all the islands in the Pacific, which it has seized or occupied since the beginning of the First World War in 1914, and that all the territories

Japan has stolen from the Chinese, such as Manchuria, Formosa, and the Pescadores, shall be restored to the Republic of China..." With Japan's World War II defeat and unconditional surrender in 1945, the Cairo Declaration became part of the country's capitulation by incorporation. The legal basis was codified in the San Francisco Treaty of 1951. The treaty, signed between Japan and 48 Allied signatories, excluded China and Taiwan.[4] Significantly, Article 2(b) stated: "Japan renounces all rights, title and claim to Formosa and the Pescadores". Further, Article 3 continued: "Japan will concur in any proposal of the United States to the United Nations to place under its trusteeship system with the United States as the sole administering authority, Nansei-shotō south of 29 degree north latitude (including the Ryukyu and the Daito Islands)". *The treaty did not specifically mention the Senkaku/ Diaoyu Islands.* The treaty implied that the US had the right to exercise all powers of administration, legislation and jurisdiction over the territory and inhabitants of these islands, including their territorial waters. In 1953, the US Civil Administration of the Ryukyus issued the US Civil Administration of the Ryukyus Proclamation 27 (USCAR 27) which defined the boundaries of Nansei-shotō "south of 29 degrees north latitude" to include the Senkakus.[5]

In the 1945 Potsdam Proclamation, the signatories affirmed that the terms of the 1943 Cairo Declaration would be carried out and limit Japanese sovereignty to the four major islands of Japan and to "such minor islands as we determine." Although the Allied powers did not specifically mention disposition of the Senkaku Islands in the territorial clause of the San Francisco Peace Treaty, they did decide to place the Senkaku Islands under US administration.[6] The term Nansei-shotō was understood by the United States and Japan to include the Senkaku Islands, which were being administered as part of the Okinawa prefecture. Significantly, the US Civil Administration Proclamation No. 27, of December 25, 1953, further defined the territorial jurisdiction of the US civil administration of the Ryukyu Islands and the Government of the Ryukyu Islands as "...those islands, islets, atolls and reefs as well as their territorial waters" within specific geographic coordinates that included the Senkaku Islands.[7] Okinawa, including the Senkaku Islands as part of the Nansei-shotō Islands, was placed under US administration and became a central anchor of the US military deployment in Asia. During the San Francisco Peace Treaty negotiations, the US and the UK agreed that Japan would retain "residual sovereignty" over Okinawa, and that the US would not require Japan to renounce its sovereignty over Okinawa. Naturally, the Japanese felt encouraged to consider the Senkaku Islands being included in the "residual sovereignty over Okinawa" since, for Tokyo, the islands were part of Okinawa.

The San Francisco Peace Treaty of 1951 affected the final outlook of territories in East Asia at the end of World War II. On September 04, 1951, delegates from over 50 countries gathered at the San Francisco

Opera House to discuss the making of a peace treaty with Japan. Signed by 48 countries four days later, on September 08, the San Francisco Peace Treaty marked the end of the war and hostilities between the signatories, and recognised Japan's sovereignty. Japan relinquished control of, or claims to, Korea, Formosa, the Pescadores, Sakhalin, the Kurils, and the islands it held in the Pacific, Antarctica, and the Spratly and Paracel Islands. More importantly, it gave the US control of the Ryukyu Islands (Okinawa) and other territories. On April 28, 1952, a little over seven months after the signing of the treaty, Japan formally regained its sovereignty. However, the treaty failed to specifically define the status of the Senkaku Islands and the Liancourt Rocks, with both not appearing in the territorial clauses as Chinese, Japanese or Taiwanese territory.[8]

When Japan defeated China in the Sino-Japanese War of 1894-95, the peace treaty specified that Japan would gain control of Taiwan and all of its contiguous islands, including the Senkakus. The various treaties that ended the Allied occupation of Japan in 1951 clearly specified that all provisions of pre-war treaties, including the 1895 agreement, were null and void, but for the fate of the Senkakus. The United States saw the Senkakus as part of the Ryukyu Islands in the wake of the San Francisco Peace Treaty with Japan.[9]

The claimants, namely Japan, China, and Taiwan, more specifically Japan and China, disagree over the first and initial discovery and effective occupation of the Senkaku Islands. Japan argues that the islands were *terra nullius* before 1895 (i.e. islands that no nation claimed sovereignty over) and "showed no trace of having been under the control of China". (*Terra nullius* is a term used in international law to describe territory which has never been subject to the sovereignty of any state, or over which any prior sovereign state has expressly or implicitly relinquished sovereignty.) Justifying this *terra nullius* status, Shimojo Masao disputes the Chinese claim over Senkaku Islands, i.e., their being a part of Taiwan when it was incorporated into Qing China, pointing out that the extent of Qing China, based on documents from that period, ended at Mount Jilongshan on Taiwan and the extent of the Ryukyu Kingdom ended at Gumishan (present-day Kumejima). Thus, the islands in between, including the Senkakus, were in a "no-man's land". In fact, Japan's contentions primarily stem out of the contemporary mode of *effective occupation* and proving *terra nullius* status. Japanese use of the term *terra nullius* appears in the "Fact Sheet on the Senkaku Islands," issued by the Ministry of Foreign Affairs of Japan in November 2012. Furthermore, to support its claim, Tokyo points out that a fisherman from Okinawa prefecture made an application for lease of these islands way back in 1884 – one year before the Japanese government adopted a Cabinet decision on January 14 to formally incorporate the islands into the territory of Japan, a few weeks before the end of the first Sino-Japanese War and the signing of the Treaty of Shimonoseki. On January 12,

1895, Prime Minister Ito Hirobumi was presented with an attachment paper under the title, "Secret No. 133: Matter Concerning the Placement of Markers." Two days later, the proposal was further brought before the Cabinet meeting on January 14, 1895, and the following resolution was adopted:

> The Home Minister has requested a cabinet decision on the following matter: the Islands, Kuba-shima and Uotsuri-shima, located north-westward of Yaeyama Islands under the jurisdiction of Okinawa Prefecture, have heretofore been uninhabited islands. Due to recent visits to the said islands by individuals attempting to conduct fishing related businesses, and that such matters require regulation, it is decided that [the islands] be placed under the jurisdiction of Okinawa Prefecture. Based on this decision, the Okinawa Prefectural Governor's petition should be approved. Since there are no disagreements on the matter, it shall proceed based on the above decision.[10]

On January 21, 1895, Japanese Prime Minister Hirobumi gave his final approval to the Cabinet decision, and the scheme of Meiji Japan to incorporate the disputed islands, planned long before, and awaiting only a decision on its timing, was now, at last, realised. The Japanese government has, to date, consistently regarded the above Cabinet decision of January 14, 1895, as the foundation of its legal basis for asserting and justifying its claim over the islands.

Fig 1.2: Senkaku Islands

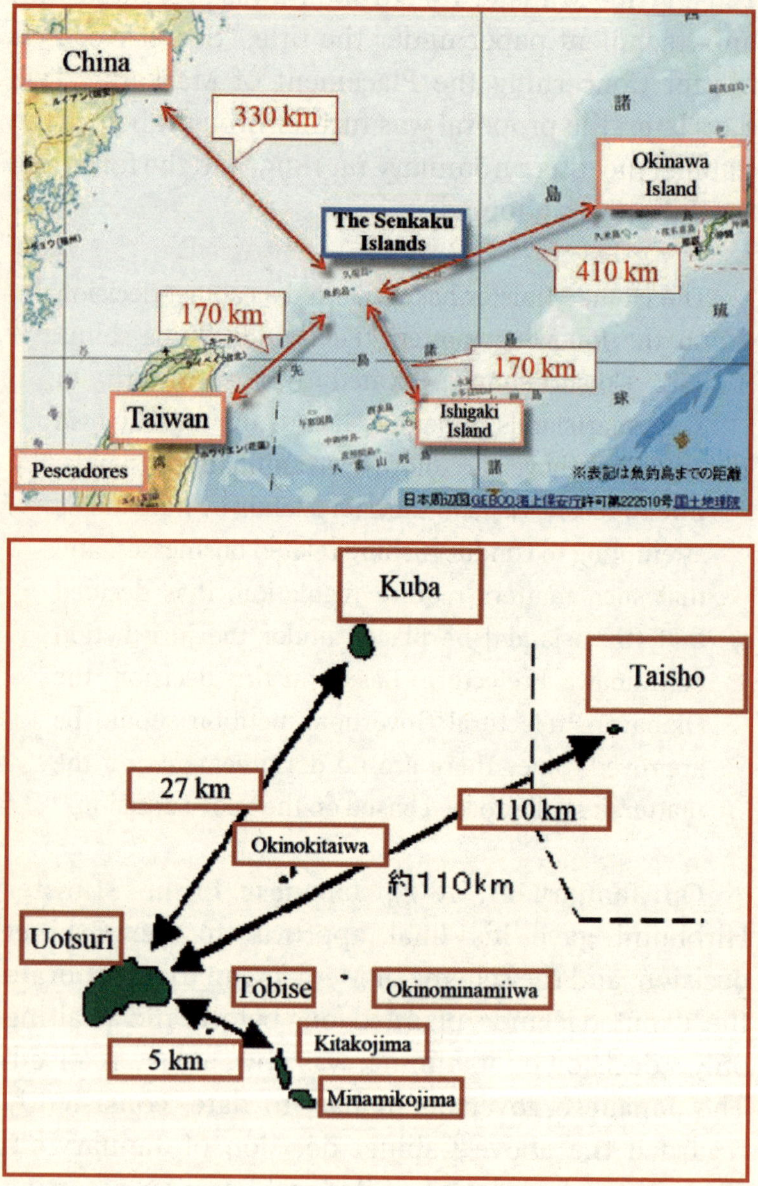

<table>
<tr><th></th><th>Ownership</th><th>Area (km^2)</th><th colspan="2">Background</th></tr>
<tr><td>Uotsuri</td><td>State</td><td>3.6</td><td rowspan="4">Leased to a Japanese citizen free of charge in 1896. Sold off to a Japanese citizen in 1932. (The ownership was then transferred between Japanese citizens.)</td><td rowspan="3">Rented out to the state on April 1, 2002. Acquired and owned by the state on September 11, 2012</td></tr>
<tr><td>Kitakojima</td><td>State</td><td>0.26</td></tr>
<tr><td>Minamikojima</td><td>State</td><td>0.32</td></tr>
<tr><td>Kuba</td><td>Private</td><td>0.87</td><td rowspan="2">Part of the US facilities and areas under the Japan-US Status of Forces Agreement since 1972.</td></tr>
<tr><td>Taisho</td><td>State</td><td>0.04</td><td>State-owned throughout</td></tr>
<tr><td>Okinokitaiwa</td><td>State</td><td>0.05</td><td colspan="2" rowspan="3">State-owned throughout</td></tr>
<tr><td>Okinominamiiwa</td><td>State</td><td>0.01</td></tr>
<tr><td>Tobise</td><td>State</td><td>0.02</td></tr>
</table>

Source: The Senkaku Islands, Ministry of Foreign Affairs of Japan, March 2013.

Japan bases its sovereignty claim on the fact that it incorporated the islands as *terra nullius* on January 14, 1895, and has been continuously occupying the islands since then. The Government of Japan incorporated the islands into Japanese territory by lawful means under the international legal framework which existed at that time. After the incorporation of the Senkaku Islands into Japanese territory, Japanese civilians settled on the previously uninhabited islands, having obtained permission from the Japanese government. Settlers ran businesses such as dried bonito manufacture and feather collecting. The islands counted more than 200 inhabitants at one point, and taxes were collected from the inhabitants. Following a January 14, 1895, Japanese Cabinet decision to put up a marker on the Senkaku Islands, the islands were formally incorporated into Yaeyama county of the Okinawa prefecture, as per repeated releases by the Ministry of Foreign Affairs, Japan. Thereafter, since 1896, they have been a part of Ishigaki city. The Japanese government originally owned the first three islands – Uotsuri, Kitakojima and Minamikojima, until 1932, when ownership was transferred to a private Japanese citizen.[11] The Japanese Ministry of Foreign Affairs issued a statement on March 08, 1972, regarding "Rights to Ownership over the Senkaku Islands." Six key assertions made in that statement are as follows:[12]

- The islands were *terra nullius* during 1885-95.
- The Japanese Cabinet decision of January 14, 1895 incorporated the Senkaku Islands into Japanese territory.
- The Senkaku Islands were *not* included in Article 2 of the Treaty of Shimonoseki 1895.
- The Senkaku Islands were *not* part of the territory which Japan relinquished under the San Francisco Peace Treaty.
- There was a legitimate transfer of title through the Okinawa Reversion Treaty, 1971.
- There was Chinese acquiescence from 1952-70.

What stands out markedly is that on an occasion in 1920, it was pointed out by a Japanese writer that the Chinese Consul in Nagasaki had mentioned the disputed islands as part of the Okinawa district of the Japanese Empire. This incident is recorded as evidence involving an emergency rescue mission perceived to be particularly persuasive in substantiating the Japanese case by means of a letter of appreciation issued by the Chinese Consul stationed in Nagasaki in 1920. The letter of appreciation thanked the people of Ishigakijima for rescuing Chinese fishermen who were washed ashore on one of the Senkaku Islands, stating that the islands are part of the Okinawa prefecture.[13] From the contents of this letter of appreciation, it is contended that the Chinese Consul, a high-ranking diplomatic official, recognised the islands as Japanese territory. This letter was first cited as evidence in the December 1972 issue of the *Okinawa Quarterly*. Subsequently, it has appeared frequently in the Japanese press, including being published as a front-page story of the September 23, 1996 *Sankei Shimbun* daily. The full letter of appreciation reads as follow:

Certificate of Appreciation by Consul of the Republic of China

> During the winter of the eighth year of the Republic of China (1919), Guo Heshun, and thirty-one other fisherman from Huei'an Prefecture, Fujian Province, were met with contrary winds and drifted to Wayo Island, Senkaku Islands, Yaeyama District, Okinawa Prefecture, Empire of Japan. With the earnest rescue by Mr. Tamaesu from Ishigaki Village, the fishermen were able to survive and return to their homeland. Deeply moved by such neighboring sympathy and willingness to perform charity without hesitance, I hereby present this certificate to express my gratitude and thankfulness.
>
> Feng Mian,
> Consul of the Republic of China in Nagasaki
> May 20th The Ninth Year of the
> Republic of China [1920]

Japan has always contended that nobody lived there until the early Meiji period (1868-1912) and argues that upon being defeated in the Sino-Japanese War, China ceded Taiwan to Japan under Article 11 of the Treaty of Shimonoseki. Japan has claimed that its incorporation of the Senkakus was an act apart from the Sino-Japanese War. China argues that Japan used its victory in the war to annex the islands and asserts that the intent of the Allied declaration at Cairo and Potsdam during World War II was to restore to China territories taken away by Japan through military aggression.[14]

Japanese-American negotiations over Okinawa sparked renewed Chinese interest in the Senkaku Islands with Chow Shu-kai, then departing Ambassador of the Republic of China (ROC), giving a 4-page aide-mémoire to US Assistant Secretary of State Marshall Green, on September 16, 1970, outlining the ROC's objections to Japanese sovereignty over these islands.[15] The White House tape of the April 12, 1971, meeting indicates Chow emphasising that the final disposition of the Senkakus should be kept open, and that this issue was a measure of the ROC's ability to protect itself, thereby highlighting the symbolic importance of the islands.[16] Interestingly, after Chow left the Oval Office, the President remarked that Chow was correct on the need to consider the political views of overseas Chinese. Chow, while further commenting on the Senkakus, remarked that even when the Japanese had occupied Taiwan and the Ryukyus, courts in Taiwan had handled legal matters involving the Senkakus.[17]

When the US started to discuss the transfer of the administrative rights over Okinawa to Japan, which led to the *Agreement between Japan and the United States of America Concerning the Ryukyu Islands and the Daito Islands* (signed June 17, 1971) the US was urged, in September 1970, not to include the Senkaku Islands, and to keep the sovereignty issue open.[18]

Finally, however, the Okinawa Reversion Treaty, signed on June 17, 1971, and ratified by the US Senate on November 10, 1971, provided for the return to Japan of "all and any powers of administration, legislation and jurisdiction" over the Ryukyu and Daito Islands, which the United States had held under the Japan Peace Treaty. Article I of the Okinawa Reversion Treaty defines the term "the Ryukyu Islands and the Daito Islands" as "all territories with their territorial waters with respect to which the right to exercise all and any powers of administration, legislation and jurisdiction was accorded to the United States of America under Article 3 of the Treaty of Peace with Japan. [...]." An agreed minute to the Okinawa Reversion Treaty defines the boundaries of the Ryukyu Islands and Daito Islands "as designated under" USCAR 27. Moreover, the latitude and longitude boundaries set forth in the Agreed Minute appear to include the Senkakus (Diaoyus) – also acknowledged by the Chinese government as well as by supporters of China's claims, who testified in the Okinawa Reversion Treaty hearings before the Senate Foreign Relations Committee. A letter of October 20, 1971, by Robert Starr, Acting Assistant Legal Adviser for East Asian and Pacific Affairs – acting on the instructions of Secretary of State William Rogers – stated that the Okinawa Reversion Treaty contained "the terms and conditions for the reversion of the Ryukyu Islands, including the Senkakus."[19]

The two principal players are contesting whether the islands reverted to China after Japan's defeat in World War II in 1945, or were restored to Japan as part of Okinawa in 1972. Documentary evidence, both historically and legally, points to suggest that the end of the American occupation of Okinawa and consequent agreement concerning the Ryukyu Islands and Daito Islands, signed by the United States and Japan on June 17, 1971, included the Senkaku Islands as part of Okinawa. Both China and Taiwan challenged the legitimacy of the transfer. Notwithstanding this, the "*United States cannot add to the legal rights Japan possessed before it transferred administration of the islands to the United States, nor can the United States, by giving back what it received, diminish the rights of the Republic of China*" (emphasis added).[20]

Japanese officials and the government at large have persistently held the view that there is no evidence, whatsoever, that either the Chinese, or anybody else for that matter, ever lived on the islands prior to the late 1800s. This accounts for the islands being historically *terra nullius*. After World War II ended, Japan returned all territory formerly belonging to China, but since China had never actually owned the islands and because the United States had administered the islands from

1945-72 as a part of Okinawa, when the US returned Okinawa to Japanese administration, the Senkaku Islands were also returned to Japanese control.[21] Towards the end of the 19th century, the region was in an amorphous transition from a Sino-centric East Asian world order to one that was increasingly dominated by Western international law. Imperial China insisted on allegiance to the former, while Meiji Japan warmly embraced the latter. "Territorial ownership" implied two very different things under these conceptual umbrellas. Chinese scholars and academics have often used it as a base to refute Japan's claims to territorial accession.[22]

That the islands were not inhabited at the time of incorporation is an oft-presented argument. Under international law, appropriation of territory is legally strengthened by making it public and by it not being contested, but notification is not an absolute condition. However, even if the islands were incorporated without this being officially made public, it must surely have come to the attention of succeeding Chinese governments that the islands were being put to use for economic purposes and inhabited by Japanese citizens, since fishermen from Taiwan and China pursuing fishing activities in the area sometimes landed there to escape storms. After Japan's incorporation of the islands in 1895, a private individual, Koga Tatsushiro used some of the islands for commercial purposes for several decades until World War II, also providing habitation for workers who were employed in his fish processing plant. Even at the beginning of the 1950s, fishermen from Irabujima near Miyakojima had stayed on Minami Kojima for up to three months to process bonito and maintained vegetable gardens. In a sudden turn of events, in 1971, China began asserting its claims of sovereignty over the Senkaku Islands. Till this time, Japanese researchers used to regularly visit the islands and used them as shelter during typhoons.[23]

China's Contending Position

The Government of the People's Republic of China (PRC) put forth its claim to the islands only in December 1971, following a report of the United Nations Economic Commission for Asia and the Far East, which mentioned a high probability of substantial oil and natural gas reserves underneath the waters surrounding the islands.[24] However, the Chinese government does not accept this and instead asserts that the islands had been controlled by China for hundreds of years since the Ming Dynasty in 1556. Founded by Zhu Yuanzhang, who later assumed the reign title of Hongwu, the Ming Dynasty, (1368-1644), which provided an interval of native Chinese rule between the eras of Mongol and Manchu dominance, led China to exert immense cultural and political influence on East Asia, the Turks to the west, and on Vietnam and Myanmar to the south. The Ming incorporated the Song Dynasty's policy of relying on the literati in managing state affairs. Although the Ming Dynasty became one of the most stable, it also earned the dubious distinction of being perhaps among the most autocratic of all Chinese dynasties. Subsequently, the Qing (Manchu) Empire took over the reins ((1644-1912) and "... in 1895, as the Qing government's defeat in the First Sino-Japanese War was all but certain, Japan illegally occupied the Diaoyu Island and its affiliated islands." Rejecting Japan's *terra nullius* claim, China contends that the Diaoyu Islands have been under Chinese jurisdiction since ancient times.[25] The Chinese claims to sovereignty over the islands are purportedly based on the following:

- The Chinese argue that a valid title was obtained through the principle of discovery-occupation as early as 1372.[26]
- There was a peaceful and continuous display of territorial sovereignty over the disputed islands for more than five hundred years (1372-1895).[27]
- Japan previously recognised and acquiesced to Chinese sovereignty over the disputed islands.[28]
- The Diaoyutai Islands were *not terra nullius* in 1895.
- The islands were ceded to Japan through the Treaty of Shimonoseki 1895.
- The islands must be returned to China under the War-Time Declarations and Sino-Japanese Peace Treaty 1952.

The Chinese acknowledge that their defeat in the first Sino-Japanese War of 1894-95 and the subsequent Treaty of Shimonoseki ceded the islands to Japan. But what is simultaneously averred is that the treaties that ended World War II clearly state that all territories seized from China before World War II would be returned to China. The government of the People's Republic of China feels that it deserves the "rightful ownership" of the islands and the official Chinese news agency, *Xinhua*, published a dispatch noting in this reference in 2012:

> Diaoyu and its affiliated islands have been considered part of China since ancient times. Chinese people were the first to discover, name and administer these islands. In June 1971, the US signed the Okinawa Reversion agreement with Japan to "return" Diaoyu and other [adjacent] islands to Japan, privately taking China's territory in a backroom deal between Japan and the US.

China's Ministry of Foreign Affairs issued a statement on December 30, 1971, pointing out that Diaoyu and its affiliated islands are an inseparable part of Chinese territory. Apparently, after the establishment of the PRC, there was an article in the state-controlled publication, *People's Daily* on January 08, 1953, which reported demonstrations in Okinawa against the US.[29]

The argument put forth by Chinese nationals is that they first discovered the islands in the 14th century, and returned later to gather medicinal herbs, and made use of the islands for navigational purposes. China quotes documents going back to the Ming Dynasty (1368-

1644), which mention the islands as part of Taiwan, although the Qing Dynasty incorporated Taiwan only in 1683.[30] Concurrently, it has been argued that fishermen from Taiwan used the islands for fishing activities since the time of the Ming Dynasty. In 1893, the Dowager Empress of China, Tze Shih, made a grant of the islands to an individual Sheng Hsuan Wai, who collected medical herbs there.[31] However, having never established a permanent settlement of civilians or military personnel on the islands, and not maintaining permanent naval forces in adjacent waters, is also an equal reality that is hard to deny and weakens the Chinese claims to the Senkaku Islands.[32]

As cited earlier in this section, the first reports about Chinese claims appeared in print in May 1970, after Japan and Taiwan started talks on jointly exploring the energy resources around the Senkaku Islands, and Okinawa's reversion was announced. Resultantly, on December 30, 1971, the Chinese Foreign Ministry published an official statement claiming the islands.[33] Not claiming sovereignty over the Senkakus till this period was a tacit acceptance by the Government of the People's Republic of China that the islands were uncontested and that Japan, in fact, controlled the islands. Academics and experts in the PRC explain China's silence by arguing that there was an absence of diplomatic relations between Beijing and Tokyo until 1972. However, the question arises, as to why would this prevent Beijing from protesting against Japan's "territorial claim to the islands", more so, on the international stage? China had been protesting against the Japanese government and its policies on many occasions, and many issues, before 1972. In addition, China's domestic instability during the Cultural Revolution (1966-69) is cited as another excuse for taking attention away from the islands. This claim by the Chinese can again be contested in that the Cultural Revolution happened for a finite period of a few years in the late 1960s. Where were the Chinese claims before that time period? What remains unclear is China's position during the treaty negotiations and in its immediate aftermath. Why did not either China or for that matter, Taiwan, protest against the inclusion of the Senkaku Islands as territories assigned to the US administration, at that very time?

Henry Kissinger was among the first to comment on the issue of hegemony, when President Nixon visited China in February 1972. This was subsequently included in the Shanghai Communiqué and read:[34]

> Neither [side] should seek hegemony in the Asia-Pacific region, and each is opposed to efforts by any other country or group of countries to establish such hegemony.

It should be noted further that the idea of "anti-hegemony" was also included at Beijing's insistence in the 1972 Japan-China Joint Communiqué, wherein Article 7 of the communiqué read:

> The normalization of relations between Japan and

> China is not directed against any third country. Neither of the two countries should seek hegemony in the Asia-Pacific region and each is opposed to efforts by any other country or group of countries to establish such hegemony.

On August 23, 1978, the Treaty of Peace and Friendship was signed in Beijing with the policy of setting aside the Senkaku dispute, which was later confirmed and reiterated in a statement made by then Vice Premier Deng Xiaoping, in a press conference during his visit to Japan on October 25, 1978. Responding to a question put forward by a Japanese reporter, Deng said:

> Our two sides agreed not to touch upon this question when diplomatic relations were normalized between China and Japan. This time when we were negotiating the Treaty of Peace and Friendship, the two sides again agreed not to touch on it... We call it Tiaoyu Island but you call it by another name. It is true that the two sides maintain different views on this opinion. It does not matter if this question is shelved for some time, say, ten years. Our generation is not wise enough to find common language on this question. Our next generation will certainly be wiser. They will certainly find a solution acceptable to all.[35]

The governments of both the PRC and Japan have constantly referred to Deng's principle of shelving the issue for the sake of the larger bilateral relationship, which indeed has also been the sole reason as to why the sovereignty issue of the Senkakus remains unresolved. In the backdrop that "administration" rather than "sovereignty" is the key distinction that applies to the islets, two primary questions need to be debated and proven, based on documentary evidence. One, whether China exercised sovereignty over the islands before 1894, and two, if, once the Shimonoseki Treaty was signed, the islands were ceded to Japan by China only to be returned after World War II.[36] While China bases its arguments on its claim to the title over the islands on the classical mode of discovery and maintaining effective occupation of the islands, it is Japan that seems closer to fulfilling all the requisite legal requirements to acquire the title over the disputed islands under contemporary international rules and law.

While presenting the Okinawa Reversion Treaty to the US Senate for ratification, when asked by the Chairman of the Senate Foreign Relations Committee how the Okinawa Reversion Treaty would affect the determination of sovereignty over the Senkakus (Diaoyus), US Secretary of State William Rogers answered, "This treaty does not affect the legal status of those islands at all."[37] The inclusion of the Senkakus (Diaoyus) in the Okinawa Reversion Treaty under the definition of "the Ryukyu Islands and the Daito Islands" made Article II of the treaty applicable to the islands, which states:

> Treaties, conventions and other agreements concluded between Japan and the United States of America, including, but without limitation, the Treaty of Mutual Cooperation and Security between Japan and the United States of America... become applicable to the Ryukyu Islands and the Daito Islands as of the date of entry into force of this Agreement.[38]

In short, while maintaining neutrality on the competing claims, the United States agreed in the Okinawa Reversion Treaty to apply the Security Treaty to the treaty area, including the Senkaku Islands. Since 1971, the United States and Japan have not altered the application of the Security Treaty to the islands.[39] The Security Treaty itself declares in Article V that each party would act "in accordance with its constitutional provisions and processes" in response to "an armed attack [...] in the territories under the administration of Japan." Therefore, it becomes increasingly vital to understand that it is "administration", rather than "sovereignty", which is the key distinction that applies to these islands.

For the dispute over the Senkaku/Diaoyu Islands, the most likely critical date is approximately 1970, however, shortly after, "whether the islands were *terra nullius*" depends upon the doctrines of occupation and inter-temporality. The former holds that a state can appropriate unclaimed territory by occupying and possessing it. The latter holds that one must judge the legality of events in the light of the law contemporaneous with their occurrence, rather than with the law in force at the time the dispute is ultimately resolved. In other words, lawful annexation by Japan requires that China had not already engaged in acts sufficient to appropriate the islands under the law of occupation that existed up to 1895.[40] For Japan, the best argument seems to be that China lost its original title by failing to update its conduct to occupy the islands within the meaning of the new doctrine. On this reasoning, pre-19th century acts by China are generally beside the point, and the acts of possession and administration in the decades leading up to 1895 were insufficient. An apparent paucity of Chinese activities in the 19th century supports this view. For example, an official PRC White Paper on the dispute mentions only an investiture mission that sailed by the islands en route to Okinawa in 1866. There is also an official gazetteer from 1871 that referenced the islands, and a series of five maps, four of which were not official publications.[41] Scholars and academics too, have found scant evidence of Chinese control.[42] However, the Senkaku Islands were unquestionably Japanese sovereign territory during the fifty years, from 1895-1945, and research has not shown any proof of China protesting against Japan's exercise of authority and occupational control over the islands from 1895-1945.

Taiwan: The Third Party to the Dispute, or Not?

In the very public and sour squabble over the Senkakus almost exclusively between Beijing and Tokyo, a third party laying claim, terming them Tiaoyutai Islands and (釣魚台), is often ignored and to a large extent, not considered a factor at all. This third party is the Republic of China (Taiwan). The Taiwanese claims get heavily weighed down with critical provisions, beginning with the fact that Taiwan is not a member of the United Nations and, consequently, does not have the right to negotiate with Japan over sovereignty issues. In September 1972, Japan officially recognised the People's Republic of China (PRC) as the only legitimate Chinese government and severed diplomatic ties with the Republic of China (ROC). This happened when in 1972, the PRC was recognised by the UN as the lawful representative Government of China. What changed ultimately for the ROC with respect to the islands dispute as a result of Japan's de-recognition, was that the sovereignty issue subsequently become a matter unresolvable through official dialogue or diplomatic means. More importantly, Beijing considers Taiwan as a renegade province of China and places it as its top most agenda in the list of Chinese "core interests".

The position of Taiwan is not essentially different to that of China. It takes the view that the Qing Dynasty was compelled to cede the islands under the Treaty of Shimonoseki of 1895 and that the Tiaoyutai Islands belonged to the island group of Taiwan. In the view of

Taiwan, the islands were returned to China after the Japanese surrender under the 1951/1952 Peace Treaties and are, therefore, currently an inherent territory of the Republic of China. Obviously, the existence of Taiwan as a separate entity next to the People's Republic of China on the mainland adds to the complexity of the issue. In fact, these are not two states, but two governments claiming to represent the same state—China. It should also be noted that Taiwan does not regard itself as a separate claimant nor can it be regarded as a separate claimant state under international law.[43]

Significantly, the "One-China" policy (一个中国; yī gè Zhōngguó) refers to the view that there is only one state called China, despite the fact that two governments claiming to be China's exist today. According to the codified 1992 Consensus, the One-China policy has been upheld by both the PRC and the ROC. Although both agree that there is only one sovereign state encompassing both mainland China and Taiwan, there is disagreement about which of the two is legitimate. Taiwan's Democratic Progressive Party (DPP), currently in power in Taipei under President Tsai Ing-wen, has often questioned as to why the international media refers to the conflict in the East China Sea only as being Japan-China- centric, and pays no heed to the Taiwanese claims. The DPP also faces condemnation from Beijing for its display of "a lack of national pride" and "flattery of Japan" over the territorial issue (釣魚台), as cited in the February 07, 2013, edition of the *Taipei Times*. It becomes only too clear that the domestic political rumblings in Taiwan are far too strong on the Senkaku issue. According to an editorial in the September 2012 issue of the publication *Lianhebao*, there appears to be a linkage between the Senkaku Islands issue and Taiwan's relationship with China per se. Chen I-hsin, a Professor of Political Sciences at the Tamkang University in Taipei, argues that the Chinese Communist Party (CCP) views the joint defence of the Diaoyu Islands as a first step towards unification. While China claims its sovereignty over these islands, claiming that they always have been part of "Chinese territory" (釣魚台自古就是中國的領土; *diaoyutai zigu jiushi zhongguo de lingtu*), the situation gets complicated with Taiwan's counter-claims. Now, the question becomes, "which China" shall prevail? While it is not hard to discern that the political spectrum within Taiwan is split on the Senkaku Islands issue in an apparent bid to gain de facto recognition as a sovereign actor from Beijing, what seems difficult to fathom is whether Taipei's internal political fissures on this issue will become too wide and complicated. In an interesting turn of events, Japan and Taiwan struck a deal in April 2013, allowing Taiwanese fisherman to use a majority of the Japanese-controlled zone around the Senkaku Islands. Although the deal was framed as an interim agreement, delaying resolution of claims of ownership, it promises to change the dynamics of the East China Sea. The agreement is aimed at furthering peace in the East China Sea, said Mitsuo Ohashi, head of the Japan Interchange Association that serves as the de facto embassy in the absence of formal diplomatic ties. The agreement covers an overlapping economic zone and does not involve areas that both sides claim as their own, Taiwanese Foreign Minister David Lin stated.[44]

While removing the main source of friction between Taiwan and Japan, it potentially creates a variety of problems for mainland China's government, which fears both diplomatic isolation on territorial issues and a revival of Taiwan's diplomatic status. The deal has significant advantages for both Taiwan and Japan in that it significantly expands the reach of Taiwan's fishermen, which is a boon for the island's economy. Besides, Japan will no longer face protests from Taiwanese fishermen – thereby pulling Taiwan toward its side of the issue. Adding to China's woes, the head of the Taiwanese Coast Guard said Taiwan's ships would help Japan to keep mainland trawlers out of the disputed area. But China also has reasons to worry about its own claim to the islands. If Japan and Taiwan can arrive at a compromise, they may well be able to cast the mainland as the unreasonable party standing in the way of resolution, thus, winning international support.[45] That said, the fact that remains unarguable is that the East Asian conflict that has long been held hostage by the bitter historical burden, is unlikely to wither away any time soon. In fact, it shall only get intensified, fanned by the flames of nationalism that shall drive the legacy of the conflict in the future.

Notes

1. For related references, see Z Pan, "Sino-Japanese Dispute over the Diaoyu/Senkaku Islands: The Pending Controversy From the Chinese Perspective", *Journal of Chinese Political Science*, Vol. 12, No. 1, 2007, p. 1.
2. The Treaty of Shimonoseki, 1895, *Treaties between China and Foreign States, Second Ed.* (Shanghai: By Order of the Inspector General of Customs), Vol. 2, 1917, pp. 590-596.
3. Caleb Wan, "Security Flashpoint: International Law and the Islands Dispute in the Far East", *New Zealand Post-Graduate Law e-Journal*, No. 2, 2005, p. 14.
4. Donatello Osti, "The Historical Background to the Territorial Dispute over the Senkaku/Diaoyu Islands", *Analysis*, No. 183, June 2013, International Peace and Security Institute, Washington D.C.
5. US Congress, Senate Committee on Foreign Relations, *Okinawa Reversion Treaty*, 92nd Congress, 1st Session, October 27-29, 1971 (Washington, U.S. Government Printing Office, 1971) (Okinawa Reversion Treaty Hearings), pp.149-152, cited in M.E. Manyin, "CRS Report for Congress Prepared for Members and Committees of Congress Senkaku (Diaoyu/Diaoyutai) Islands Dispute: US Treaty Obligations", January 2013.
6. Seokwoo Lee, "The 1951 San Francisco Peace Treaty with Japan and the Territorial Disputes in East Asia", *Pacific Rim Law and Policy Journal*, Vol. 11, No. 1, 2002, p. 89.
7. Ibid.
8. Ibid.
9. Daniel A Metraux, "The Senkaku Islands Dispute between China and Japan", *Southeast Review of Asian Studies*, Vol. 35, 2013, p. 222.
10. Ryukyu Government, "Reference 3: Official Documents", *History of Okinawa Prefecture*, Vol. 13, 1967, p. 593.
11. Akira Kato, "The United States: The Hidden Actor in the Senkaku Islands", *Asia Pacific Bulletin*, No. 205, April 02, 2013, East West Center, Honolulu (HI).
12. Published by *The Japan Times Online* 2004; for related reference,

also see Wan, n. 3, p. 18; and see Reiji Yoshida "Is the Senkaku Row About Nationalism, or Oil?" *The Japan Times*, March 27, 2004.

13. The text of the entire communication is available at http://www.mofa.go.jp/region/asia-paci/senkaku/pdfs/fact_sheet_03.pdf ; also see Okuhara, "Senkaku Retto to Ryoyuken Kizoku Montai" (The Problem of the Right of Sovereignty Over the Senkaku Island), *Asahi Asian Review*, No. 22, 1972; and Official Release by the Japanese Ministry of Foreign Affairs; and see "Japan-China Relations Surrounding the Situation of the Senkaku Islands in Response to China's Airspace Incursion", *Gaimusho, Position Paper*, December18, 2012; also see S. Wei, "The Territorial Dispute over the Tiaoyu/Senkaku Islands: An Update", *Ocean Development & International Law*, Vol. 36, No. 1, 2005.
14. Okinawa Reversion Treaty Hearings, "The Diaoyutai Islands An Inherent Part of the Territory of the Republic of China (Taiwan)," Ministry of Foreign Affairs, Republic of China (Taiwan), available at http://www.mofa.gov.tw/EnOfficial/Topics/TopicsArticleDetail/fd8c3459-b3ec-4ca6-9231-403f2920090a, pp. 149-152; also, see Larry A Niksch, "Senkaku (Diaoyu) Islands Dispute: The US Legal Relationship and Obligation," *Asian Affairs*, Foreign Affairs and National Defense Division, United States Congressional Research Service, September 30, 1996; Tao Cheng "The Sino-Japanese Dispute Over the Tiao-yu-tai (Senkaku) Island and the Law of Territorial Acquisition", *Virginia Journal of International Law*, Vol. 14, Winter 1974, pp. 248-249.
15. As cited in, National Archives, RG 59, EA/ROC Files: Lot 75 D 61, Subject Files – Petroleum – Senkakus, January-September 1970.
16. Ibid. Also see *Nixon Presidential Materials*, White House Tapes, recording of conversation between Richard Nixon and Henry Kissinger, April 12, 1971, Oval Office, Conversation No. 477-3.
17. For more details, see *China*, January-September 1971; Memorandum [102] from the President's Assistant for National Security Affairs (Henry Kissinger) to President Nixon, Washington, January 12, 1971; also see Memorandum of Conversation between Henry A. Kissinger

(Assistant to the President for National Security Affairs), Chow Shu-kai (Departing Ambassador of the Republic of China), and John H. Holdridge (Senior Staff Member, NSC), Washington, April 12, 1971.

18. *Foreign Relations of the United States (FRUS),* Vol. XVII (1969-1976), p. 292, available at http://2001-2009.state.gov/documents/organization/70142.pdf
19. According to the Okinawa Reversion Treaty Hearings, 91st Congress; and see Niksch, n. 14.
20. As was communicated via a *Telegram*, cited in a State Department File, (2946) State Department Records, Record Group 59, June 17, 1971; on file with the US National Archives and Records Administration.
21. For more details, see Metraux, n. 9, p. 221.
22. Reinhard Drifte, "The Senkaku/Diaoyu Islands Territorial Dispute between Japan and China: Between the Materialization of the China Threat and Japan 'Reversing the Outcome of World War II'?" *UNISCI Discussion Papers,* No. 32, May 2013, p. 12; also see, Han-yi Shaw, *The Diaoyutai/Senkaku Islands Dispute: Its History and an Analysis of the Ownership Claims of the PRC, ROC, and Japan* (Baltimore: University of Maryland School of Law, 1999), pp. 64-68; particularly the quoted Chinese complaint in the 1870s during the negotiation about Okinawa, cited on p. 66.
23. "A Home Away From Home / Fishermen Worked, Took Shelter, Grew Vegetables on Senkakus", *Yomiuri Shimbun*, July 07, 2012; also see Anthony Reedman and Yoshihiko Shimzaki, *A World of Difference: Forty Years of the Coordinating Committee for Geoscience Programmes in East And Southeast Asia, 1966-2006* (Bangkok, September 2006), p. 43.
24. For more details, see Committee for Coordination of Joint Prospecting for Mineral Resources in Asian Offshore Areas, *Technical Bulletin,* Vol. 2, Geological Structure and Characteristics of the East China Sea and the Yellow Sea, pp. 39-41, 1969.
25. As cited in the Statement of the Ministry of Foreign Affairs of the People's Republic of China, September 10, 2012, available at http://www.fmprc.gov.cn/eng/topics/diaodao/t968188.htm

26. Tsui Hsueh, "Tsung Shih Liu Chiu Lu Kan Tiao-yu-yu" (To View the Diaoyu Tai Through the 'Mission to the Ryukyu Records), *Sinological Studies*, Vol. 2, 1972, p. 48.
27. Cheng, n. 14, p. 221, 259.
28. Fung Hu Hsiang, "Evidence beyond Dispute: Tiaoyutai is Chinese Territory", cited in William B Heflin "Recent Developments Diaoyu/ Senkaku Islands Dispute: Japan and China, Oceans Apart", *Asian-Pacific Law & Policy Journal*, Vol. 1, 2000, pp. 18, 21.
29. As per the Statement of the Ministry of Foreign Affairs of the People's Republic of China, Ministry of Foreign Affairs of the PRC, September 10, 2012, available at http://www.fmprc.gov.cn/eng/ topics/diaodao/t968188.htm
30. Shaw, n. 22, pp. 42-69.
31. Peter N. Upton, "International Law and the Sino-Japanese Controversy Over the Territorial Sovereignty of the Senkaku Islands", *Boston University Law Review*, Fall 1972, p. 767; also see n. 5, pp. 89-90.
32. Cheng, n. 14, pp. 244-246; also see Upton, Ibid., and see R Jade Harry, "A Solution Acceptable to All? A Legal Analysis of the Senkaku-Diaoyu Island Dispute," *Cornell International Law Journal*, Vol. 46, No. 653, 2013.
33. Tatsuo Urano, ed., *Diaoyutai qundao (Senkaku Shoto) wenti, Yanjiu ziliao huibian* (Hong Kong: Lizhi Chubanshe, 2001), pp. 35-36; also see *People `s Daily*, May 18, 1970, and December 29, 1970, editions.
34. Joint Communiqué of the USA and the People's Republic of China 1972, (*Shanghai Communiqué*) (Published February 28, 1972.)
35. As cited in the *Peking Review*, No. 44, November 03, 1978, p. 16.
36. Osti, n. 4, pp. 4-5.
37. Niksch, n. 14, p. 63.
38. Ibid., p. 64.
39. Ibid.
40. For more details, see Ryan M Scoville, "A Defense of Japanese Sovereignty over the Senkaku/Diaoyu Islands", *Legal Studies Research Paper Series*, No. 13-16 (Wisconsin: Marquette University Law School, June 2013).

41. "Diaoyu Dao: An Inherent Territory of China," State Council Information Office of China, October 23, 2012, available at http://ma.china-embassy.org/fra/xwdt/t981801.htm
42. For in-depth research on this subject, see Greg Austin, *China's Ocean Frontier: International Law, Military Force and National Development* (Allen & Unwin Publishers, 1998), pp. 164-167; and also see Scoville, n. 40.
43. For more details, see Alfred Soons and Nico Schrijver, "What Does International Law say About the China-Japan Dispute Over the Diaoyu/Senkaku Islands?", *Briefing Paper*, The Hague Institute for Global Justice, December 03, 2012, pp. 14-15.
44. David Cohen, "Japan and Taiwan's Senkakus Play," *The Diplomat*, April 13, 2013.
45. Ibid.

2. International Law, Legal Provisions, and Conventions

With territorial disputes spread far and wide across the world, international law has, over centuries, evolved and developed rules for determining claims that are lawfully sovereign, or in other words, the "title to territory" of a nation state over a particular territory, which is in dispute. Notwithstanding this practice, many times it becomes rather impossible to determine the strength of the claim/claims in the absence of complete verifiable access to all relevant materials and historical records.

Multilateral Conventions and Protocols

For legal parties in territorial disputes, there is no general international convention on the acquisition of territory or how to assess the value of one nation's claim of sovereignty over another nation's competing claim. Despite the gaping holes in the international law of territorial title, there are international conventions governing island and maritime law once the issue of sovereignty is settled. Although the existing covenants and protocols on the Law of the Sea can do little to dispel any doubts or ambiguities about territorial title, they can certainly be helpful in elucidating the importance of the Senkaku/Diaoyu Islands dispute to the countries involved, as well as to the international community. First, the 1958 Geneva Convention on the Continental Shelf (GCCS) was a major covenant governing the Law of the Sea for many years and was still in effect when the dispute over the Senkaku/Diaoyu Islands first began to build steam. The GCCS is a relatively brief and limited document, but is notably clear on the rights to an island's adjoining seabed. Since then, however, the cumbersome two hundred-page United Nations Convention on the Law of the Sea (UNCLOS) has replaced the Geneva Convention on the Continental Shelf. UNCLOS today is the only convention currently codifying sovereignty rights for island territories.[1] Article 121(1) of the Law of the Sea Convention defines an island as "a naturally formed area of land, surrounded by water, which is above water at high tide."

The respective positions of the states involved herein differ again, with China regarding them as "rocks", whereas Japan takes the position that they are proper "islands" and entitled as such to an Exclusive Economic Zone (EEZ) and continental shelf of their own. UNCLOS provides both Japan and China with a 12 nautical-mile (22 km) zone of sovereignty from its coast and an EEZ that extends till 200 nautical miles (370 km) from the baselines from which the breadth of the territorial sea is measured and not beyond. In addition, giving the state sovereign rights to resources in the water column, the seabed, and a continental shelf, where it exists, over which states have rights over the seabed up to 350 nautical miles from the coast. However, the geographical size of the EEZ raises a number of issues in that those relatively smaller bodies of water (referred to as "rocks" in this provision), less than 400 miles, that cannot sustain human habitation or economic life of their own, could see a substantial overlap between the EEZs of two or more countries. The possibility of maritime jurisdictional zones overlapping requires delimitation of a maritime boundary between the states involved. For instance, the East China Sea measures 360 miles across at its widest point. Despite the high likelihood of an overlap, UNCLOS (Article 121, paragraph 3) does not provide any clear directive to address this aspect.[2] Thus, it is only established that owing to the lack of a convention on territorial acquisition and the ambiguities surrounding UNCLOS, the law in this realm does little to elucidate sovereignty disputes, particularly surrounding the Senkakus.

Customary Law states that, historically, five modes of territorial acquisition have emerged as mechanisms by which countries legally acquired territory: (1) discovery and occupation; (2) conquest; (3) prescription; (4) cession; and (5) accretion. The first element, discovery, largely depends on the absence of prior claims on the territory. Accordingly, the territory must be *terra nullius*. The second element, effective occupation, consists of two additional sub-elements: first, the nation must exhibit the intention to act as a sovereign; and, second, the nation must also exercise actual sovereign authority.[3] Though the islands are volcanic rock formations, accretion is a theory that is unlikely to bolster either China's or Japan's claims for sovereignty since all volcanic growth of the Senkaku/ Diaoyu Islands probably occurred before any claim to the islands was made. Discovery and occupation comprise the most likely avenue for both countries to claim sovereignty and in reference to both, discovery and occupation, the strongest argument stands in favour of Japan. This holds in the light of Japan incorporating the islands as vacant territory, and its effective control, which went unchallenged for a very long time. Bolstering the Japanese claim under discovery and occupation comes in the wake of Tokyo discovering the Senkaku Islands when they were still *terra nullius*, while there is no evidence that China ever established settlements or occupied the islands as a colony.

For that matter, Chinese maps during the American trusteeship of the islands refer to the islands by their Japanese name, suggesting that China did not believe that it had ownership of the islands directly following World War II. A number of Chinese maps predating the 1960s, refer to the Diaoyu Islands by their Japanese name – Senkaku. Since 1971, Japan has held the islands, as the United States did, in a trusteeship. Thus, whether or not there is possession or occupation in the legal sense, there is clearly some degree of possession or control over the islands in the more general sense and, of course, "possession is nine-tenths the law." Additionally, the Security Treaty between Japan and the United States, requiring the United States to respond to any invasion of the Senkaku Islands, further corroborates the fact that Japan has some form of possession of the islands, as no other nation could occupy the islands without first piercing an American military defence. In addition to Japan's possession of the islands as an administrator, Japan also likely intended to act as a sovereign over the Senkakus following the transfer of administrative rights.[4]

Terra Nullius Concept and Status

While deliberating on the contesting claims over the Senkaku/Diaoyu Islands, rules of contemporary international law, most importantly establishing the *terra nullius* positional concept, bear immense significance. *Terra nullius* is a Latin term meaning "land belonging to no one / no-man's land". In this reference, it could be a volcanic island, a territory abandoned by a former sovereign, or a territory that is not possessed by a community belonging to a social and political organisation. Consequently, this allows a state, but not a private individual, to acquire territory, which belongs to no one – excluding areas constituting *res communis* (common heritage of mankind). This mode of acquisition primarily relates to "uninhabited territories and islands" but *terra nullius* may be established if the territories inhabited by tribes or peoples did not demonstrate a social and political organisation.[5] Derived from *occupation* in Roman law, the word occupation "does not necessarily signify occupation in the sense of actual settlement and a physical holding."[6] With respect to international law, there are two major categories in which the issue could be classified: (1) the dispute over the sovereignty of the islands themselves; and (2) the implications of the dispute on maritime jurisdiction. While the former deals with the question of how sovereignty may be obtained over the islands, the latter deals with issues such as the possibility of generating extended maritime zones under the UN Convention of the Law of the Sea.[7] The UNCLOS defines an EEZ as "an area beyond and adjacent to the territorial sea, subject to the specific legal regime established in this Part, under which the rights and jurisdiction of the coastal State and the rights and freedoms of other States are governed by the relevant provisions of this Convention." Furthermore, "[I] n the exclusive economic zone, the coastal State has . . . sovereign rights for the purpose of exploring and exploiting, conserving and managing the natural resources . . . of the waters superjacent to the seabed and of the seabed and its subsoil."[8]

However, Article 121(2) of UNCLOS goes on to say that "rocks which cannot sustain human habitation or economic life of their own shall have no exclusive economic zone or continental shelf," which becomes a taxing clause in the case of the Senkaku/Diaoyu Islands' rock-like characteristics and absence of human settlement. Legal experts and commentators have expressed the opinion that the Senkaku/Diaoyu Islands, are indeed, islands, with full rights to the potentially valuable EEZ circling the islands.

In the study of the law on territorial acquisition, public international law advocates that the state is the primary type of legal person. A legal person is a subject of the law – meaning that it is "an entity capable of possessing international rights and duties and having the capacity to maintain its rights by bringing international claims."[9] Sovereignty, on the other hand, can be described as the competence of states in respect of their territory. Internally, sovereignty may be expressed as the "supremacy of the governmental institutions" and, externally, as the "supremacy of the state as a legal person."[10] While possession of territory is the prime criteria for establishing statehood, with the state being the foundation of international law, the concepts of sovereignty, state and territory are inseparable.[11] It, thus, only becomes germane that the concept of territorial sovereignty is regarded as the fundamental axiom of classical international law, and a foundational principle whereby a state is deemed to exercise full and exclusive authority over its territory.[12] This covers land territory, the territorial sea appurtenant to the land, the seabed and subsoil of the territorial sea, islands, islets, rocks and reefs. When a state claims sovereignty over a territory, it is asserting ownership and possession over it. Besides, another essential element of occupation is "effective possession" which refers to a combination of two criteria also borrowed from Roman law: "the material apprehension of a corpus and the manifestation of *animus possidendi* (intention to act as sovereign)."[13]

In international law, "discovery becomes legally relevant when a state affirms that the discovery was made on its behalf and proceeds to claim territorial sovereignty."[14] Discovery of *terra nullius* alone does not grant actual title to the discoverer. Discovery only conveys inchoate title, which requires more concrete acts of actual occupation or exercise of authority to demonstrate sovereignty over an island. Even with physical occupation, a state must demonstrate acts of sovereignty by peaceful and continuous performance rather than merely an intention to claim sovereignty over the area.[15] Though claims to uninhabited islands require exercising less authority over the island to maintain a title than an inhabited island, a sovereign must still timely protest the acts of other competing sovereigns that constitute occupation or the exercise of state functions, or that sovereign risks losing the title altogether. Second, no amount of historical or documentary evidence will trump the actual long-term, peaceful occupation or the exercise of state authority over a territory in controversy. Last, besides actual occupation, the International Court of Justice (ICJ) or an arbitrator will also consider whether the parties involved essentially concurred to the other state's occupation of an island.[16]

International Law

When Japan conducted official surveys of the Senkaku Islands in 1883 and 1887, and, subsequently, made a Cabinet decision on January 14, 1895, to erect a marker on the islands and incorporate them formally into Japan, China did not put up any official/public protest against any of these actions. At the end of World War II, the Ryukyu Islands and surrounding areas in the East China Sea (including the Senkaku/Diaoyu) were occupied by the American forces. These areas were then incorporated into the United States Administrative Area under Article 3 of the San Francisco Peace Treaty of 1951. As a result of the bilateral agreement between the United States and Japan, the Okinawa Reversion Treaty of 1971 returned the disputed islands to Japanese control. Japan jointly patrolled and administered the Senkakus with the United States, and post-1972, Japan continued to patrol the islands and surrounding EEZ unilaterally, while building and maintaining a heliport and navigational lighthouses – thus, establishing Japan's operational exercise of actual physical sovereignty. Under contemporary international law, the controlling legal principle regarding sovereignty over an uninhabited island is the peaceful and continuous exercise of authority.[17] Japan for sure, has a more persuasive and cogent case by virtue of its peaceful and continuous exercise of authority over the islands, which China did not protest/contest timely.

The requirements of international law regimes, particularly the UNCLOS, which was ratified by Japan and the PRC in 1996, prompted both countries to take domestic and/or international administrative and legal steps, for instance, passing legislation related to the administration of their maritime space, demarcating their sea borders, and claiming borders for their EEZ. These had a general purpose but did not sufficiently take into account the need to protect the bilateral understanding of putting the territorial dispute aside. Both countries must always consider that whatever is decided in relation to the Senkaku Islands might have implications for the country's other territorial disputes [Japan's territorial disputes with the Republic of Korea over the Liancourt Rocks (Takeshima) and with Russia over the Kuril Islands chain; China's EEZ dispute with the Republic of Korea and territorial disputes with the other littoral claimants in the South China Sea.][18]

When China passed the Law of the People's Republic of China on the Territorial Sea and the Contiguous Zone or simply the Territorial Law, and adopted it at the 24th meeting of the Standing Committee of the Seventh National People's Congress on February 25, 1992, the first two Articles drew immediate attention, and predictable controversy...

Article 1

> The Law is enacted for the People's Republic of China to exercise its sovereignty over its territorial sea and the control over its contiguous zone, and to safeguard its national security and its maritime rights and interests.

Article 2

> The territorial sea of the People's Republic of China is the sea-belt adjacent to the land territory and the internal waters of the People's Republic of China. The land territory of the People's Republic of China includes the mainland of the People's Republic of China and its coastal islands; Taiwan and all islands appertaining thereto, including the Diaoyu Islands; the Penghu Islands; the Dongsha Islands; the Xisha Islands; the Zhongsha Islands and the Nansha Islands; as well as all the other islands belonging to the People's Republic of China. The waters on the landward side of the baselines of the territorial sea of the People's Republic of China constitute the internal waters of the People's Republic of China.[19]

The Japanese government, naturally, protested vehemently over the explicit inclusion of the Diaoyu Islands.[20] At that point in time, the Japanese government was preoccupied in preventing China's global isolation as an aftermath of the 1989 Tiananmen crackdown. For this reason, China too, played down the impact of this law and went back to refer what Deng Xiaoping had stated in 1978 – to leave the resolution of the territorial issue for the future generations. When Jiang Zemin visited Japan in April 1992, he reaffirmed the shelving according to Deng's promise in 1978, while still restating China's claim to the islands. However, it has often been cited that the Chinese Ministry of

Foreign Affairs (*Waijiaobu*) originally did not want to include the Senkaku Islands, since including them undermined the strength of the shelving agreement, dating the start of the process leading to the ultimate breakdown of the shelving agreement to around this time.[21]

When it ratified UNCLOS in 1996, China referred to the abovementioned 1992 law and promulgated the precise location of its baselines, but left out a few of them, including those for the Senkaku Islands. Subsequently, in 1998, China's National People's Congress promulgated the PRC Exclusive Economic Zone and Continental Shelf Act, which also failed to mention any specific geographical areas. Clearly, the Chinese leadership was trying to walk a fine line between its territorial and EEZ claims (including the need to respond to domestic demands, increasingly dominated by nationalist tendencies), and the requirements of the international law regime.[22] Concurrently, Japan also ratified UNCLOS in June 1996, and established in the following month the Law on the Territorial Sea and the Contiguous Zone, as well as the Law on the EEZ and Continental Shelf, which were supplemented by guidelines for implementation. The latter also established an EEZ around the Senkaku Islands. Japan did not include the Senkaku Islands into its straight baseline claim. Two separate Bills creating the Basic Law of the Ocean and the Law on Establishing Safety Areas for Maritime Structures were passed by the Japanese Diet in April 2007, and came into effect on

July 16, 2007. The latter two laws were passed mainly having in mind any future exploitation of natural resources in the contested EEZs. Unsurprisingly, China does not recognise the validity of these laws for the Senkaku Islands, or for the EEZ border between the two countries. And by virtue of this, the dispute remains a primary obstacle for agreement on the EEZ border in the southern area of the East China Sea, which is not made easier by the fact that an agreement on the title to the Senkakus would have a major impact on the size of the EEZ area of the successful claimant.[23]

For the first time since 2004, when non-Japanese nationals landed on the Senkaku Islands, the Japanese police resultantly arrested them on August 15, 2012. The group of 14 pro-China activists set sail from Hong Kong. If an arrest is sufficient to constitute an investigation of criminal activity or hold judicial proceedings, then a court of law could well hold that Japan did, in fact, exercise actual sovereign authority over the islands. On the one hand, if a court viewed the purchase of the islands as an outright purchase, this would surely diminish Japan's authority as a sovereign as it would suggest that Japan was purchasing sovereign rights that it did not already have. However, based on Japanese Foreign Minister Kōichirō Genba's opinion-editorial, Tokyo is likely to argue that the purchase of the islands was not, in fact, a purchase of the territory, but rather a nationalisation of the islands. In other words, it would be similar to a situation where the United States purchased the Hawaiian Island of Lanai. Although all the Hawaiian Islands are American territory, in order to claim the Lanai Island of this group, as government property, the United States would have to purchase and nationalise the island from its current private owner, Larry Ellison (who bought 98 percent of the island, with the remainder being government property, and private homes).

It is imperative to note here that the issue of private ownership of the islands is not relevant to resolving the sovereignty question. The sale by the Japanese private owners of the property of some of the islands to the Japanese state, which triggered the latest eruptions of public emotion in China and Taiwan, does not at all affect their status under international law. Under Japanese law, after their takeover by Japan in 1895, the islands had been sold to private owners for economic exploration and management. However, the title to sovereignty to the islands can only rest with a state, and should not be confused with the issue of private property rights.[24] Moreover, the issue of private and state ownership of the Senkaku Islands, which falls under the headings of international law, needs to be carefully understood. In 1896, Koga Tatsushiro obtained a free lease of 30 years for the islands of Uotsurijima, Kubajima, Minami Kojima and Kita Kojima. Following the death of Koga Tatsushiro in 1918, his son, Koga Zenji, took over the business on the islands. In 1926, following the end of the free lease, the Japanese government converted it to a rental basis.[25]

In 1932, the Japanese government changed the

status of these four islands from state-owned to privately-owned land by selling them to the Koga family. After 1945, Kubajima and Taishojima (the latter was always state-owned) were leased to the US to be used as firing ranges. In 1972, Koga Zenji sold Kita Kojima and Minami Kojima, followed by Uotsurshima in 1978, and Kubajima in 1988, to Kurihara Kunioki, a real estate investor, and his family. In 2002, Kitakojima, Minami Kojima and Uotsurijima were leased to the state, which paid 25 million Japanese yen per year as rent. The US military used Kubajima and Taishojima from 1957 as firing ranges, and after the reversion of Okinawa in 1971, continued to do so until 1979 by paying rent to the private owner of Kubajima; however, post 1971, the rental payment was effected by the Japanese government.[26] Since the shelving of the territorial issue in 1972 and 1978, the islands changed private owners, and the state rented three of the islands from their private owner and owned one. The leasing in 2002 coupled with the "nationalisation" (with no money involved) of the Uotsurijima beacon in 2005 resulted in Chinese protests. What needs to be highlighted is that the private ownership changes did not surprisingly, and moreover, shockingly, cause any Chinese reaction.

The principal rule of international law, embodied in Article 2(3) of the United Nations Charter and elaborated in Article 33, states that disputes between states must be resolved by peaceful means by virtue of direct negotiations between the parties. In negotiations, the states involved are entirely free to define the considerations they would want to play a role. Any resolution they agree on should ideally be acceptable in case it does not affect the rights of a third state nor is contrary to international law. Should the states involved not be able or willing to undertake direct negotiations, a third party (for example, another government, private person or international organisation) may offer, or be requested by them, to play a facilitating role, either by providing (passive) good offices or by (active) mediation.[27] The resolution reached with the assistance of the third party would eventually still be reflected in an agreement between the disputing states. A further option is that the parties decide to request a person or commission to suggest a proposal to resolve the dispute, called "conciliation", which involves the possibility of basing the resolution on policy considerations, rather than on the applicable rules of international law.

However, past practice shows that in these diplomatic means of settling disputes the (perceived) relative strengths of claims under international law also inevitably play a role in the process.[28] The basic rule of international law applicable in this case is that maritime boundaries beyond the territorial sea must be established by agreement in order to achieve an equitable solution. This usually means a three-phase approach: (1) an equidistance line is drawn provisionally between the (island) coasts of the two states; (2) an assessment is made of whether there are relevant circumstances, which are mostly related to coastal geography, requiring an adjustment of the provisional equidistance line; and (3) a determination will be finalised if the resulting line is "equitable", meaning that it does not lead to a disproportional attribution of maritime areas to one of the states. If that is considered to be the case, the equidistance line will be adjusted accordingly. Any line that the two states agree upon is regarded as being "equitable" provided it does not affect the rights of third states.[29]

Under the international Law of the Sea, coastal states can claim a continental shelf beyond 200 nautical miles when certain geological conditions are met. China claims a continental shelf from the mainland extending to the east of the islands, while Japan claims an EEZ/continental shelf extending to the west of the islands, up to the median line with China's mainland coast. Resultantly, the two states also have a dispute on the location of their maritime boundaries in the area. If the two states cannot reach an agreement through negotiation, the same rules apply as described above with respect to submitting the dispute to an international court or arbitral tribunal. However, this can only be done with the consent of both parties involved. It should be noted that in 2006, China opted out of compulsory dispute settlement provisions with respect to maritime delimitation under the UNCLOS. Japan has not made use of the option to exclude such disputes.[30] On September 13, 2012, Beijing submitted a nautical chart with baselines of the territorial sea on

Senkaku Islands to the United Nations, and announced on September 16, that it was going to submit its Partial Submission Concerning the Outer Limits of the Continental Shelf beyond 200 Nautical Miles in the East China Sea to the Commission on the Limits of the Continental Shelf under the UNCLOS – which is a plan to request the natural extension of China's continental shelf to the Okinawa trough, thus, including the Diaoyu/Senkaku Islands.[31] This was seen as an attempt to bolster its claim "to the right to claim the undersea continental shelf beyond the normal 200 nautical miles because it is a 'natural prolongation' of China's land territory" into the East China Sea. Following this diplomatic assertion, China launched a force aggression when its marine surveillance planes were reported in the air space near the islands in December 2012, to be confronted by Japanese fighter jets over the East China Sea. China, seemingly is putting into application, all means available, be it a flawed legal argument, historical reference, or, for that matter, propping up the nationalist sentiment/card to garner support and momentum over its supposed claim on the Senkaku Islands.

Notes

1. United Nations Convention on the Law of the Sea, opened for signature on December 10, 1982, Article 121(1) 21 I.L.M. 1261, 1291; for related references, see R. Jade Harry, "A Solution Acceptable to All? A Legal Analysis of the Senkaku/Diaoyu Island Dispute," *Cornell International Law Journal*, Vol. 46, No. 653, 2013, p. 106.

2. Ibid., pp. 110-115; also see, Alfred Soons and Nico Schrijver, "What Does International Law say About the China-Japan Dispute Over the Diaoyu/Senkaku Islands?", *Briefing Paper*, The Hague Institute for Global Justice, December 03, 2012, p. 13; Professor Alfred Soons is Chair of Public International Law and Director of the Netherlands Institute for the Law of the Sea, Utrecht University; and, Professor Nico Schrijver is Chair of Public International Law and Academic Director of the Grotius Centre for International Legal Studies, Leiden University.
3. Harry, n. 1, pp. 117-121.
4. Ibid., pp. 170-171.
5. Malcolm N Shaw "The Western Sahara Case", *British Yearbook of International Law*, Vol. 49, 1978; also see Han-yi Shaw, *The Diaoyutai/Senkaku Islands Dispute: Its History and an Analysis of the Ownership Claims of the PRC, ROC, and Japan* (Baltimore: University of Maryland School of Law, 1999), p. 425.
6. Caleb Wan, "Security Flashpoint: International Law and the Islands Dispute in the Far East," *New Zealand Post-Graduate Law e-Journal*, No. 2, 2005, p. 9.
7. Jon M Van Dyke, "Legal Status of Islands – With Reference to Article 121(3) –The UN Convention of the Law of the Sea" (1999), University of Hawaii, Faculty of Law.
8. n. 1.
9. Ian Brownlie, *Principle of Public International Law*, 6th ed. (Oxford Press, 2003), p. 57.
10. For more details, see Malcolm N Shaw, *International Law*, 5th ed., (Cambridge Press, 2003), p. 409.
11. Wan, n. 6, p. 6.
12. Shaw, n. 10.
13. For more details on this subject and conceptual narratives, see Paul O'Shea, "Sovereignty and the Senkaku/Diaoyu Dispute", Stockholm School of Economics, *Working Paper*, No. 240, September 2012, p. 6; also see Carlos Ramos-Mrosovsky, "International Law's Unhelpful Role in the Senkaku Islands," *University of Pennsylvania Journal of International Law*, 2009, p. 906.

14. Santiago Torres Bernardez, "Territory, Acquisition" in R Berhardt, ed., *Encyclopaedia of Public International Law* (North Holland, New York, 2000), Vol. 4, p. 832.
15. Ibid., p. 836.
16. William B Heflin, "Diaoyu/Senkaku Islands Dispute: Japan and China, Oceans Apart", *Asian-Pacific Law & Policy Journal*, Vol. 18, No. 1, 2000, Hawaii, pp. 98-102.
17. Ibid., p. 120.
18. Reinhard Drifte, "The Senkaku/Diaoyu Islands Territorial Dispute Between Japan and China: Between the Materialization of the 'China Threat' and Japan Reversing the Outcome of World War II", *UNISCI Discussion Papers*, No. 32, May 2013, p. 23.
19. *Law of the People's Republic of China on the Territorial Sea and the Contiguous Zone,* Standing Committee of the National People's Congress, Order of the President, People's Republic of China, No. 55, February 25, 1992.
20. Takashi Okada, *Senkaku shoto mondai* (Tokyo: Sososha, 2012), p. 102.
21. Akio Takahara, "The Senkaku Trawler Collision Incident" (at the time of writing, this book was being published) in Mike Mochizuki, ed., *The Okinawa Question: Regional Security, the US-Japan Alliance, and Futenma* (Washington, D.C.: Sigur Center for Asian Studies, 2011), p. 3.
22. Drifte, n. 18, pp. 23-24.
23. Ibid.
24. Soons et al., n. 2.
25. Unryu Suganuma, *Sovereign Rights and Territorial Space in Sino-Japanese Relations: Irredentism and the Diaoyu/Senkaku Islands*, (Honolulu: Association for Asian Studies and University of Hawai'i Press, 2000), p. 119.
26. As translated from the report, "*Nihon to taishaku keiyaku*", *Sankei Shimbun*, September 21, 1996; also see, Drifte, n. 18.
27. Soons et al., n. 2, p. 15.
28. Ibid.
29. Ibid., p. 16.

30. Ibid., p. 17.
31. "China to Submit Outer Limits of Continental Shelf in East China Sea to UN", *Xinhua* News Agency Press, September 16, 2012, available at http://www.china.org.cn/world/2012-09/16/content_26538076.htm

3. The Resurgence of Nationalism in China and Japan

The resurgence of nationalism in the post-Cold War era, has given rise to three broad themes in literature. The first focusses on the use of nationalism to divert attention from the state's inability to meet societal demands for security, economic development and effective political institutions.[1] Regimes may seek to bolster their grip on power by blaming foreigners for their own failures, increasing international tensions.[2] The second looks at groups within the state that have expansionist or militarist goals. By propagating nationalist or imperialist myths, they can generate broad public support for their parochial interests.[3] And, the third emphasises upon how political elites can spur nationalism to gain an advantage in domestic political competition. Nationalism can be used both to mobilise support for threatened elites and to fend off potential challengers. Political institutions aim to channel popular participation and reconcile contending claims.[4] All three approaches focus on nationalism's instrumental value, seeking to gain or hold onto power by promising fulfilment of popular nationalist demands. Nationalism can not only aggravate ethnic relations within the state, but can also spill over borders and increase the likelihood of international conflict.[5]

Nationalism as a reverberating factor in East Asian politics needs to be comprehended in the light of the domestic political scene of the countries concerned. Driven by the symbolic significance of the Senkaku Islands, state-supported nationalist irredentism is widely visible. Mark Valencia argues adroitly that the primary reason for diplomatic, political and strategic tensions surrounding the Senkaku Islands dispute to be rising every now and then is not because of oil, but because of "unresolved historical grievances and the politics of national identity."[6] The strong wave of nationalism prevalent in both China and Japan is a factor that has upgraded itself to perhaps becoming among the primary drivers for domestic political wrangling on the sovereignty claims over the Senkaku Islands. Nationalism, a long history of war, revulsion and mistrust have long characterised Sino-Japanese relations. Weighed down by heavy historical baggage, the dispute over sovereignty of the Senkaku Islands only further complicates the situation. The Chinese leadership's actions in the decade of the 1990s' Diaoyu Islands dispute graph, witnessed leaders promoting nationalist and anti-Japanese sentiment to increase their domestic legitimacy and mobilise public sentiment on the issue.

Chinese Nationalism

China plays its nationalism card very well with the Chinese Communist Party (CCP) continuing to make use of appeals to a militant form of popular nationalism that emphasises its own central role. The strong nationalist sentiment has hardened the regime's position when it comes to maritime disputes, particularly over the Senkaku Islands.[7] The Chinese government has perennially cited the significance of territory and territorial nationalism. Beijing's typical approach to anti-Japanese popular nationalism is two-fold: maintaining an unyielding position on Japan while restraining popular actions at home when they appear to damage the larger national interest. For instance, during the anti-Japanese demonstrations in April 2005, Premier Wen presented a tough government line in an interview, when he urged Japan to "face up to history squarely", or it could not "take greater responsibility in the international community", thus, hinting at Japan's bid for a permanent UN Security Council seat.[8] In order to placate public anger and deflect anti-establishment challenges, the government has to maintain a hardline policy towards Japan. This is why Chinese popular nationalism has been a primary factor causing bilateral tensions at the official level. There is a predominant belief that Japan is indebted to China. Having been exposed to the history of Japanese atrocities presented in minute detail, stark acerbity and frequent exaggeration, the general public in China has developed enormous grievances as well as a strong sense of entitlement towards Japan.

During the 19th century, the balance of power in world politics shifted decisively towards the West. Expansionism in Asia was at its peak. As a result of the Opium War, the Anglo-Chinese Treaty of Nanjing (1842) was signed requiring the Chinese government to pay Yuan (Renminbi) 6 million for the opium, Yuan 3 million (Renminbi) to the merchants and Yuan 12 million for the expenses incurred.[9] The Treaty of Nanjing is usually referred to as the "first unequal treaty" in the modern history of China. Subsequently, the Chinese were forced to sign, what they term as various "unequal treaties" of cession, including the Treaty of Tianjin 1858, the First Convention of Beijing 1860, and the Second Convention of Beijing 1898. Later, with the weakening of Marxist, Leninist and Maoist ideologies the world over, and the collapse of Communism in Eastern Europe and the Soviet Union, the Chinese leadership was driven to introspect and make up for the loss of Communism's political ideology with a burgeoning economic graph that would ensure continued rule of the Chinese Communist Party. Beijing has managed to weave the Diaoyu issue into the historical narrative of Japan's refusal to repent for its past aggression. According to Zheng Wang, the CCP "... has used history education as an instrument for the glorification of the party, for the consolidation of national identity, and for the justification of the political system of the CCP's one-party rule in the post-Tiananmen and post-Cold War eras".[10] This has ensured that more than six decades after the war, the enmity of the past remains alive in today's younger generations.[11] Another prominent Chinese scholar puts it across more simply and states, "... The main theme of Chinese nationalism is anti-Japan".[12]

The Japanese often perceive that Chinese public opinion towards Japan is monolithically negative. The reasons for the Chinese public's negative views on Japan are not very surprising. Does anti-Japanese public opinion benefit the Chinese government? The process of public opinion formation is different in an authoritarian regime from that in a democratic one.[13] Recall when German-American political scientist Hans J. Morgenthau famously stated, "... the rational requirements of good foreign policy cannot, from the outset, count upon the support of a public opinion whose preferences are emotional rather than rational."[14] Although China's political leaders continue to employ socialist rhetoric, the search for normative arguments that can legitimise the CCP's rule has led them in two potentially incompatible directions. The first emphasises nationalist goals and highlights the Party's success in building China into a powerful state; the second emphasises economic goals and claims that the political stability provided by CCP rule is necessary for continued economic growth. The Qing Dynasty's inability to resist Western and Japanese imperialism caused Chinese intellectuals to turn to nationalism as a means of mobilising the energies of the Chinese people to "save China". The development of Chinese nationalism in this context has given sovereignty and territorial integrity intense symbolic value.[15] The CCP has sought to shape the character of Chinese nationalism drawing selectively on Chinese history to meet the political and strategic needs of the moment. In a sense, the term "nationalism" is used both to refer to government efforts to appeal to pre-existing nationalist sentiment, and to deliberate attempts to stir up nationalist sentiment for political ends.[16]

Anti-Japanese sentiment and its mobilisation in the PRC are complex and multi-faceted, and need to be viewed in the light of the elite struggle amongst the Chinese leadership. The PRC is not a monolithic institution, and its politics is characterised by a highly personalised series of conflicts over policy issues. During the period of Deng Xiaoping's preeminence (1978-96), there was push for a rapid and perhaps radical reform, centred around Deng himself and his close supporters such as Hu Yaobang, Zhao Ziyang and Jiang Zemin and the more moderate (or perhaps conservative) reformers, centred around Chen Yun and his close supporters such as Li Peng and Deng Liqun. As conflict over the direction of the reform between these groups oscillated, so did government pronouncements about relations with Japan and the mobilisation of nationalism.[17]

The first outburst of popular repugnance to Japan occurred in the mid-1980s when Chinese university students staged demonstrations in several big cities protesting against Japanese Prime Minister Yasuhiro Nakasone's official visit to the Yasukuni Shrine, the

Japanese textbook distortion of war history, and the dumping of Japanese goods in the Chinese markets.[18] In 1987, an overseas Chinese journal first published an article by an influential political dissident, Fang Lizhi, which sounded out disapproval of the Chinese policy to renounce war reparations. "After the war, Japan ought to pay China war reparation in hundreds of billions of dollars", he said, "but with the consent of Premier Zhou (the debt) was cancelled by one single stroke of writing".[19] Since then, anti-Japanese mass demonstrations have routinely become a political concern on anniversary days of the war or in times of bilateral diplomatic disputes. On the eve of Japanese Prime Minister Ryutaro Hashimoto's visit to China in September 1997, the government mobilised Party cadres to "dissuade students from demonstrating" against his worship at the Yasukuni Shrine.[20] The redressal movement resonated so much amongst not only the general public but also government officials, that it prompted Beijing to circulate a red-letter headed document among cadres at the departmental and Army level on the eve of the National Day in 1992, warning them "not to raise, encourage others to raise, and support any attempt to claim indemnity against Japan as the Japanese emperor is about to visit China".[21]

Both history and international relations theory suggest that a rising power's challenge to a declining hegemon often results in war, be it passive or active.[22] This structural concern is heightened by the popularity of a number of nationalist tracts, as well as recent aggressive Chinese military actions that have stimulated talk of a "China threat". Former President Jiang Zemin, National People's Congress Chairman Li Peng and, Prime Minister Zhu Rongji employed both nationalism and economic performance in their efforts to restore the domestic legitimacy of the CCP. Domestic legitimacy and international behaviour have a reciprocal relationship, and in that symbiosis, Chinese bigots are promoting a new variety of nationalism with an explicitly expansionist character.[23]

The legitimacy of the CCP has always rested on its nationalist credentials, while contemporary Chinese nationalism has been profoundly shaped by the Chinese experience at the hands of what they term as "Japanese imperialism". In a way, Chinese nationalism and anti-Japanese sentiment have become fused over the past decades.[24] Suisheng Zhao, one of the foremost commentators on the new Chinese nationalism, has succinctly highlighted the reason for this by stating, "The rapid decay of Communist ideology has led the CCP to emphasise its role as the paramount patriotic force and guardian of national pride in order to find a new basis of legitimacy."[25] A nationalist text titled *The China that Can Say No*, gained considerable notoriety as it contained several strong criticisms of Japan.[26] Besides, books such as Wang Junyan's *Guard Against Japan: Yesterday's Invasions and Today's Expansion*, published in 1996, were direct attacks on Japan, both its historical role in Asia and its current practices.[27]

General improvements in the economic situation

can substitute for improvements in personal economic circumstances for a while, but tolerance of inequality does not last indefinitely. Survey data indicate that Chinese citizens view growth in economic inequality and "pocketbook issues" such as inflation, job security and social services as important measures of government performance.[28] Since Tiananmen, China's leaders have tried to forge a new ideological connection between economic performance and legitimacy by arguing that political stability is an essential precondition for economic development. The Chinese Communist Party has emphasised a development-oriented neo-authoritarianism that claims that authoritarian rule is necessary during the early stages of economic development.[29] The argument that the CCP is the only force capable of holding China together, and guiding economic development, has proven persuasive and credible to many Chinese.[30]

Ideally, the CCP would like to maximise its legitimacy by making strong appeals for nationalism while simultaneously raising living standards, but power constraints and the contradictions between domestic appeals to nationalism and a development strategy that relies heavily on foreigners mean that trade-offs exist between nationalism and economic performance. Chinese officials often seem to be confronted in that too much of any nationalistic response might turn into anti-government sentiment, leading to protests and possible revolt. The general strategy of the CCP has been to allow anti-Japanese protests, which divert political frustrations to Japan rather than the government, but then, call them off soon afterwards in order to prevent them from spiralling into anti-government protests. Peter Gries notes that since "popular nationalism can threaten the Party's legitimacy, it is an increasingly significant constraint on China's Japan policy."[31]

A vital constraint that prevents Chinese leaders from leaning too heavily on either nationalism or economic performance is China's international power position, which limits its ability to attain nationalist objectives that could potentially involve use of force/military. Excessive nationalism can stir up demands for assertive international policies that Chinese leaders cannot presently satisfy. Another constraint is domestic reactions in that if Chinese leaders push nationalism so far that it interferes with economic growth, it is likely to increase unemployment and popular discontent. In order to exploit both sources of legitimacy in a complementary manner, the government seeks to shore up its nationalistic credentials through propaganda aimed at a domestic audience while simultaneously sending reassuring messages about China's desire for international cooperation to foreign audiences. Even if diplomatic agreements to shelve disputes do not prejudice China's future negotiating position, failure to pursue its claims aggressively when nationalistic issues arise, damages the regime's nationalist credentials.[32] The 2002 publication of an article by Ma Licheng, a Chinese liberal intellectual, "New Thinking on Relations with Japan," in which Ma criticised anti-

Japanese popular nationalism and argued that the Chinese government should make more efforts to improve Sino-Japanese relations was provocative. Once Ma published this view, he was immediately "cursed as a 'traitor' on various Internet chat rooms for being soft on Japan." When Shi Yinhong, another Chinese intellectual and a political scientist, defended Ma's position from the perspective that China should improve Sino-Japanese relations in order to balance "hegemonic" American power, he too, faced intense criticism by the public on the Internet. Ma's and Shi's arguments generated powerful debates among scholars and experts, which suggested that there was plurality among the elites on Chinese views toward Japan. The government was facing plural views from academic experts and a monolithic view from popular nationalists.[33]

The recent rise in Chinese nationalism is partly the product of the regime's conscious efforts to craft a new ideology that can justify the continued rule of the CCP. Chinese political leaders are rational actors who balance the need to maintain domestic legitimacy with the pursuit of longer-term international objectives. Although pressure from the military or factions within the CCP that favour a more aggressive pursuit of nationalist goals has sometimes affected Chinese foreign policy, the argument presented is that civilian control and cautious behaviour that balances economic and strategic objectives comprises the norm.[34] Japan, without doubt, has played a central role in the rise of

Chinese nationalism, both as a spur for the development of Chinese state patriotism and as a target for Chinese xenophobia. Japan's military victory in the 1895 Sino-Japanese War and its subsequent takeover of Taiwan and Korea have been portrayed to be humiliating because the Chinese have traditionally considered Japan to have a derivative and inferior culture. Japan's invasion of China in the 1930s and war-time atrocities such as the 1937 Nanjing Massacre gave rise to popular anti-Japanese sentiment that continues to resonate widely. Chinese nationalists have used the Senkaku dispute to rekindle resentment of Japanese militarism and the Nanjing Massacre to refresh the memory of historical injustice meted out to millions of Chinese. This is evident in Chinese nationalist literature like *The China that Can Still Say No.*[35]

In fact, the CCP's initial claim to legitimacy rested largely on its role in organising resistance to Japan.[36] The Chinese leadership has been able to use the issue of Japan's war-time behaviour to portray China as a victim and keep Japan perennially on the defensive. Although these tactics have been effective, growing concerns about aggressive Chinese behaviour and structural changes in the Japanese political system may be diminishing Japan's tolerance for Chinese nationalism.[37]

Will anxiousness surrounding the future course of Chinese nationalism prove true when nationalism, in its interaction with rising Chinese power could well produce aggressive behaviour? Perhaps what the Chinese leadership fails to foresee is that in the domestic context of nationalism, which manifests as popular indignation against Japan, the attempt to combine nationalism with a pragmatic foreign policy to promote China's modernisation conflicts may eventually become a threat to domestic stability within China.[38] The Chinese leadership might well face the challenge of popular nationalism turning from a tool into a threat and eventually becoming a double-edged sword.[39] While the rising nationalist sentiment may, to some extent, facilitate social mobilisation and solidify popular allegiance to the state, anti-foreign nationalism can undermine Beijing's diplomacy towards Western countries aimed at securing a stable inflow of foreign investment and technology as well as cultivating China's image as a peaceful and responsible player in the international community. The dilemma that Beijing is facing between domestic political concerns and foreign policy goals has prompted some Chinese policy elites to explore other potentially constructive solutions.[40]

Anti-Japanese nationalism in China, particularly visible in anti-Japan protests taking place in Beijing, Guangzhou, Jinan, Qingdao, Shanghai, Shenzhen and Xian, became a prominent wave in its nationalism discourse during the decade of the 1990s. Earlier, in Mao's era and during the Cold War, China had enough domestic issues to be resolved, including the class struggle and confrontation between the CCP and the Kuomintang. For the remaining part, Mao was known to incite the nationalist sentiment against "international threats", namely, the US and, later, the erstwhile Soviet Union, to consolidate the CCP's position at home.[41] As far as Taiwan's recent history goes, as a colony of Japan for 50 years, an outpost of the losing side in the Chinese civil war determined to "reclaim the mainland" and then as an increasingly democratic polity lacking significant international recognition, it has created a complex series of conflicting conceptions of the 'nation' among the people who live on Taiwan. To further complicate these issues is a series of ethnic and sub-ethnic cleavages, and the amorphous nature of what it may mean to be "Chinese".[42] Many Taiwanese begin to regard their Taiwanese identity as more significant than (or, indeed, as existing, instead of) their Chinese identity. It is this Taiwanese consciousness that begins to manifest itself as Taiwan nationalism. The Kuomintang (KMT), over the past 15 years, has become a "Taiwanese" party rather than a party dominated by the interests of the group of "mainlanders" who fled to Taiwan with Chiang Kai-shek in 1945.[43] The Diaoyutai are of great symbolic significance to the progressive and liberal Democratic Progressive Party (DPP; 民主进步党) and other opposition groups because of the importance of demonstrations over the islands in the early period of the democracy movement. Initially inspired by the KMT, the "Protect the Diaoyutai Movement" (*Bao Diaoyutai Yundong*) soon gained a momentum of its own and developed into a major intellectual movement that addressed the broader questions of Taiwan's status and political circumstances.[44]

Having normalised diplomatic relations with Japan in 1972, Premier Zhou Enlai told Japanese delegates that there was no need to mention the Diaoyu Islands, which did not count as a problem of any sort compared to recovering normal diplomatic relations.[45] Six years later, in 1978, Deng Xiaoping visited Japan in the first ever visit by a PRC leader and proposed that China and Japan should shelve the territorial dispute in order to improve their bilateral relationship. In 1984, Deng reiterated that China's domestic development couldn't be interrupted by territorial disputes, which should be shelved and replaced by developing "joint exploitation".[46] However, by then, the first display of public anti-Japanese nationalism sentiment had started to surface with the first Sino-Japanese textbook controversy of 1982.[47] It was the first time since the war that China had taken issue with Japan's historical views and to appease the conservative faction's critique of the shift from class struggle to economic modernisation and to dampen the growing social instability and the declining public faith in the CCP, Deng seized the opportunity to boost Chinese patriotism. From 1985 onwards, a campaign by the Ministry of Education emphasised the teaching of China's history of resisting foreign aggression and after the Tiananmen debacle in 1989, Japan was targeted as a "national enemy".[48]

Nationalism or, in official Chinese parlance, "*patriotism*" (*aiguo zghuyi*) replaced Maoism-Marxism-Leninism as the foundation of the Chinese Communist Party's legitimacy to enhance internal cohesion. In 1992, the National People's Congress promulgated a law on the "Territorial Sea and the Contiguous Zone" – in which, the geographic scope of China's sovereignty claim included, among others, the Diaoyu Islands in the East China Sea.[49] Thus, while the rise of anti-Japanese nationalism since the early-to-mid 1980s was part of the Deng leadership's efforts to dampen the opposition to the shift from class struggle to economic modernisation, similarly, China's post-Deng leaders have often used anti-Japanese nationalism to shore up the CCP's legitimacy.[50] While China increases its overall national and military strength, the patriotic and nationalistic sentiments have also grown and the Chinese public is quite unhappy with what they claim as Tokyo distorting history to spread the "China threat" fallacy, conniving with Taiwanese secessionists, and engaging in disputes with China over territorial and maritime interests.[51]

Japanese Nationalism

Rising nationalism that initially was restricted strictly to right wing Japanese political discourse seems to have come a long way since World War II, when nationalism in Japan was widely denounced and debated. Japanese nationalism has been traced back by historians to the Tokugawa era, which began in 1603. However, it was only during the Meiji period (1868-1912) that Japanese nationalism took on its contemporary form. After 1945, nationalism was relegated to the fringes of Japan's popular debate—at least, until recently. This marginalisation was a result, in large part, of Japan's "fear of itself." Memories of the humbling surrender by the Japanese high command aboard the US battleship *Missouri* and the devastation and shock in the aftermath of the nuclear bombing at Hiroshima and Nagasaki further fuelled this syndrome.[52] The fresh wave of nationalism is not an unalloyed trend in Japan. The "new nationalists" in Japan have become a key constituency for the structural reform of the nation and its economy, especially those in the business community, as they support strong corporate governance and realise the primary goal of the nationalists – that is, to regain Japan's leadership position in the world. The database of the *Asahi Shimbun*, one of the leading national dailies, revealed a sudden rise since the beginning of 2014, in the number of articles that included the term *ukeika*, meaning "tilt to the right."

The campaign *Bao Diao* (Protect the Diaoyu) notably in Taiwan and Hong Kong, led to Japanese political right and other nationalistic groups taking up the issue as a symbol of nationalism. Way back in 1973, several right wing politicians/law-makers within the ruling Liberal Democratic Party, including Shintaro Ishihara, joined the anti-Communist *Seirankai* or "Blue Storm Group". The Diet Association for the Preservation of Territorial Integrity was established in 2004 and in March of the same year, the Security Committee of the Lower House passed a resolution on preserving territorial integrity and demanded a stronger Japanese stance. In fact, it was the first time that the Diet passed a resolution relevant to the Senkaku Islands.[53] In a large public demonstration in Shinjuku, central Tokyo, in the Spring of 2012, in front of Odakyu Department Store, pamphlets were distributed stating that the Senkaku Islands are sovereign Japanese territory, further accusing China of coveting the islands and castigating the "weak" Japanese government for not showing any backbone in confronting the Chinese over the issue.[54]

In Japan, a new wave of nationalism appeared in both the ruling and opposition camps, with conservative tendencies deepening, coupled with arguments for guarding against, and containing, China, gaining ground. Japanese nationalism, especially the far-right, ultra-nationalist Japanese groups, notably the Nihon Seinensha, have been central in driving the dispute ever since they helped to precipitate the 1978 crisis when the Sienensha were clearly working with the support of anti-China groups of the right wing of the Japanese LDP. Although, the Seinensha may be a minor political force, it signals the emergence of a more assertive nationalism campaign in Japan. Particularly important is the symbolic recognition of the Hinomaru 'Rising Sun' flag as the Japanese national flag and recognition of the 'Kimigayo' as the Japanese national anthem. These shifts have great symbolic significance, as both have been associated in Japan and overseas, with the period of Japanese imperialism and military expansion. For that matter, the legacy of the war with China is a divisive issue in Japan with no clear consensus on the issue of Japan's responsibilities. The Japanese nationalist-revisionist line on China is well represented by Edo Yusuke, who argues that the PRC's position over the Senkaku Islands is part of an expansionist agenda by the Chinese leadership designed to dominate the sea-lanes in East Asia and simultaneously threaten Japan.[55]

Tokyo Governor Ishihara Shintaro announced in April 2012 that the Tokyo Metropolitan Government was negotiating the purchase of three of the four privately held Senkaku Islands — Uotsuri, Kitakojima and Minamikojima — by the end of the year. The lease of the central government for these three islands was due to expire in March 2013.[56] Taken aback by Ishihara`s surprise move, the Chief Cabinet Secretary, Fujimura Osamu declared the following day that the central government might acquire the islands "if required", and Prime Minister Yoshihiko Noda implied in a Diet speech on April 18 that purchase by the central government was one of the options.[57] In a meeting on May 18, Noda and his top advisers decided in principle to purchase the islands.[58] The Noda administration reportedly paid Yen 2.05 billion ($26 million) for the islands, with the Japanese Cabinet approving the use of reserves from the fiscal year's budget for the purchase. The central government initially estimated the value of the three islands at around Yen 500 million, however, with Governor Shintaro Ishihara and the Tokyo Metropolitan Government collecting more than Yen 1.4 billion in contributions from the public for its bid, the central government was forced to counter with an offer of about Yen 2 billion.[59] The immediate fallout came in the form of Chinese political counter-measures ranging from cancellation of official and unofficial visits, to further legal acts in order to reinforce China's claim to the Senkaku Islands. Around 40 percent of ceremonial events in Japan to mark 2012 as the 40th anniversary of the normalisation of diplomatic relations with China were cancelled or postponed.[60] Besides, China's Meteorological Administration started providing weather forecasts for the entire Senkaku area on the state-run TV stations.[61]

In the cyber realm, websites of nearly 19 Japanese banks, universities and other institutions came under cyber attack.[62] At a demonstration in Shanghai, about 7,000 protesters chanted slogans such as "Beat Japanese imperialism", "Boycott Japanese products" and "Destroy Japan and retrieve Okinawa."[63] On the other hand, in a survey conducted by the *Mainichi Shimbun,* 82 percent of respondents said that the Japanese government had not protested strongly enough to Beijing over anti-Japan protests.[64] In the third week of September, "Nippon Gambare", a right wing organisation chaired by former Air Self-Defence Force Chief Tamogami Toshio, staged a march through parts of Tokyo. In other cities, a brief fire was started at a Chinese school in Kobe and two smoke bombs were thrown into the Chinese Consulate General in Fukuoka.

The strategic tension with China, most significantly, in the past few years over the Senkaku Islands, has strengthened the hands and sentiments of Japanese nationalists who think their country should once more possess the military power to rival that of its neighbours. The result of these shifts has been that various nationalist positions that were once considered radical are no longer thought of as being outlandish. Akira Maeda, a law Professor at Tokyo Zokei University, argues, perhaps correctly, that the territorial disputes that flared up recently have fuelled a burst of nationalist sentiment across Japan.[65] China's growing military might and assertiveness added to this phenomenon. Japanese academics, currently Professors at Kyoto, Terumasa Nakanishi and Kazuya Fukuda, believe that the best way for Japan to avoid being the target of North Korean nuclear missiles is for the Prime Minister to declare without delay that Japan will arm itself with nuclear weapons. Besides, this sentiment appears regularly in *The Sankei Shimbun*, Japan's nationalist daily (with a circulation of over two million). The nationalist pitch for acquiring nuclear weapons was strong in mid-2002, when Chief Cabinet Secretary Yasuo Fukuda argued publicly that the Constitution did not prevent Japan from acquiring nuclear weapons. Ichiro Ozawa, the head of Japan's Liberal Party, also chimed in, asserting that Japan could counter any Chinese threat by producing "three to four thousand nuclear warheads.[66]

Former Chief Cabinet Secretary Fukuda's comments were echoed by Tokyo's Governor, Shintaro Ishihara, who perhaps, till date, remains Japan's most well-known nationalist. Given his growing popularity, Ishihara became so powerful that the LDP decided to endorse him in an April 2003 election – despite the fact that he was an independent candidate. Not surprisingly, Ishihara won approximately 70 per cent of the vote in that race, the highest margin ever for a Tokyo Governor. Ishihara is best known among the "new nationalists". Having won the Japanese equivalent of the Booker Prize at the age of 23, Ishihara co-authored (with the late Akio Morita, co-founder of the Sony Corporation) one of the most contentious books in post-war Japanese history, titled *The Japan That Can Say No*. The book, which was published in 1989 and sold over a million copies, is a stream-of-consciousness nationalist manifesto, in which Ishihara and Morita argue that the United States needs Japan as much as, or more than, Japan needs the United States. Being an independent – having shunned the LDP – Ishihara has done a great deal to popularise Japanese nationalism, allowing many ordinary Japanese to embrace the cause of self-reliance without shame.[67]

On September 14, 2003, Prime Minister Koizumi called for a national debate on the issue of amending Article 9 of the Japanese Constitution (which came into effect in May 1947), which essentially commits the country to pacifism under this clause by prohibiting an act of war by the state. The Article also states that armed forces with war potential will not be maintained. Ishihara has long supported the revision of Article 9, arguing that for Japan to be more independent, it must have a strong military. Some politicians, who publicly bristled at his more outlandish statements, are now acknowledging Ishihara's nationalist playing field. They value him as a catalyst for the kind of change that Japan needs if it is to reemerge globally. Domestically, Japanese politicians have also recognised that if Ishihara has managed to break the monopoly that the LDP has on power, other reform-minded politicians, both inside and outside the LDP, are likely to benefit. Further fuelling the nationalistic fire is the more conservative, right wing stance taken by the present Prime Minister Shinzo Abe, who not only ensured his eventual return to power in September 2012, but has also been promoting the theme around the world that "Japan is back". Abe's rightist language dates back to his first term as Prime Minister in 2006-07 and again in December 2013, just short of a year into his second administration. In addition, mid-August 2014 saw Japanese Cabinet ministers and more than 80 law-makers visiting the Yasukuni Shrine, seen by critics as a symbol of Japan's past militarism. In the current context, Prime Minister Shinzo Abe is expected to continue to press for Cabinet approval of a "reinterpretation" of the war-renouncing Article 9 of the Constitution. Many within the ruling LDP have sought to amend Article 9 for decades.[68] The debate in the Lower House of the Japanese Diet is raging over the LDP presenting a draft amendment to Article 9, with Prime Minister Shinzo Abe consistently arguing that the current interpretation of Article 9 of the Constitution makes it difficult to protect Japanese citizens in a changing security environment. The lawmakers have identified one key question: would the Self-Defence Forces (SDF) be allowed to use force on another nation's territory in support of the US military? Under the pacifist and war-renouncing Constitution, Japan has long upheld a self-imposed rule that it must only defend its own country. Armed units of the SDF should never be deployed to use force overseas because it would exceed the "minimum necessary self-defence" as allowed under the post-war Constitution. However, recent Diet sessions have heard Abe insist repeatedly that he will stay within this limitation. But, at the same time, the Abe administration is introducing new Bills that allow Japan to exercise the right of collective self-defence, or the right to come to the aid of an ally under attack, aimed at bolstering the Japan-US military alliance.[69]

Nationalism in Japan might portend a movement away from its previous method of conducting international policy, namely, "cheque book diplomacy," leading to a fierce debate about the future of Japan's foreign policy options.[70] Moreover, the public in Japan has grown weary of the apologies its successive governments have been continually pressured into making over the nation's past behaviour before and during World War II. It is not entirely true, reasonable, or fair, to state that the Japanese government and the people have avoided responsibility for the past. In fact, in 1995, on the 50th anniversary of the end of World War II, then Japanese Prime Minister Murayama Tomiichi issued a statement apologising for Japan's past colonisation and aggression, in the form of a Cabinet decision. What is significant is that subsequent administrations have continued to adhere to it.[71] The Japanese now feel that their country has apologised enough for the actions 70 years ago and is it about time Tokyo started afresh and moved away from perpetual diffidence.

As H. Richard Niebuhr writes in *The Meaning of Revelation*, "...where common memory is lacking, where people do not share in the same past, there can be no real community, and where community is to be formed, common memory must be created . . . the measure of our unity is the extent of our common memory."[72] Further, George Orwell wrote in his *Notes on Nationalism*, "... the nationalist not only does not disapprove of atrocities committed by his own side, but he has a remarkable capacity for not even hearing about them." The extent to which Japan and China ultimately interpret their respective history will have an impact upon the actions and policies of the present governments in the two capitals and, consequently, an impact directly on the nationalist fabric prevailing in East Asia that will goad the politico-military strategy of the region. Besides, the economics of nationalism too merit attention in that economic reform has had differential impacts in rural and urban areas, and in coastal and interior provinces.[73] Resulting in a rapid increase in economic inequality, it underscores the economic significance of the Senkaku Islands, as discussed in the following chapter.

Notes

1. Jack Snyder, "Nationalism and the Crisis of the Post-Soviet State" in Michael E Brown, ed., *Ethnic Conflict and International Security* (Princeton, NJ: Princeton University Press, 1993), pp. 79-101, cited in Erica S Downs and Phillip C Saunders, "Legitimacy and the Limits of Nationalism: China and the Diaoyu Islands," *International Security*, Vol. 23, No. 3, Winter 1998/99, pp. 114-146.
2. Stephen Van Evera, "Hypotheses on Nationalism and War," *International Security*, Vol. 18, No. 4, Spring 1994, pp. 30-33.
3. For more details, see Jack Snyder, *Myths of Empire: Domestic Politics and International Ambition* (Ithaca, NY: Cornell University Press, 1991).
4. Edward Mansfield and Jack Snyder, "Democratization and the Danger of War", *International Security*, Vol. 20, No. 1, Summer 1995, pp. 5-38.
5. Downs and Saunders, n. 1.
6. Mark J. Valencia, "The East China Sea Dispute: Context, Claims, Issues, and Possible Solutions", *Asian Perspective*, Vol. 31, No. 1, 2007, p. 157.
7. For more details, see Suisheng Zhao, "Foreign Policy Implications of Chinese Nationalism Revisited: The Strident Turn", *Journal of Contemporary China*, Vol. 22, No. 82, 2013, pp. 535-553.
8. For more details, see Yinan He, "History, Chinese Nationalism and the Emerging Sino-Japanese Conflict," *Journal of Contemporary China*, Vol. 16, No. 50, February 2007, pp. 1-24.
9. For more details, see John S Gregory, *The West and China Since 1500* (New York: Palgrave Macmillan, 2003), pp. 76-87.
10. Zheng Wang, *Never Forget National Humiliation* (New York, 2012), p. 8; also see Ming Wan, *Sino-Japanese Relations: Interaction, Logic, and Transformation* (Washington DC, 2006), p. 150.
11. Ibid., pp. 209-210.
12. "Dangerous Waters: China-Japan Relations on the Rocks," *Asia Report*, n. 245, April 08, 2013, International Crisis Group, Beijing/ Brussels.

13. Hiroki Takeuchi, "Sino-Japanese Relations: A Japanese Perspective" in Niklas Swanstrom and Ryosei Kokubun, eds., *Sino-Japanese Relations: Rivals or Partners in Regional Cooperation?* (Singapore: World Scientific Publishing Co. Ltd., 2013), pp. 38-39.
14. Hans J Morgenthau, *Politics Among Nations: The Struggle for Power and Peace*, 2nd ed., (New York: McGraw-Hill, 1985).
15. Downs and Saunders , n. 1.
16. Ibid.
17. Phil Deans, "Contending Nationalisms and the Diaoyutai/Senkaku Dispute", *Security Dialogue*, Vol. 31, No. 1, March 2000, pp. 119-131.
18. Allen Whiting, *China Eyes Japan* (Berkeley: University of California Press, 1989); Akihiko Tanaka, *Nitchu Kankei 1945-1990* [Sino-Japanese Relations: 1945-1990] (Tokyo: The University of Tokyo Press, 1991), pp. 137-139, and pp. 150-152.
19. For a Japanese translation of the article, see Lizhi Fang, "*Nihonjin no Seizai no Senso¯kan ni Tsuite*" ['Regarding the latent war view of the Japanese people'] *Chu¯o Ko¯ron*, 1987, pp. 172-178.
20. "China: Students Urge PRC's Declaring Stand on Japan Issues", *Hong Kong Ping Kuo Jih Pao*, September 03, 1997, as cited in Foreign Broadcast Information Service (hereafter FBIS-CHI), pp. 97-246.
21. "Indemnity Claims During Emperor's Visit Discouraged," *Hong Kong Ming Pao*, October 02, 1992, FBIS-CHI, pp. 92-192; for more details, see Yinan He, "History, Chinese Nationalism and the Emerging Sino-Japanese Conflict", *Journal of Contemporary China*, Vol. 16, No. 50, February 2007, pp. 1-24.
22. Paul M Kennedy, *The Rise and Fall of the Great Powers: Economic Change and Military Conflict from 1500 to 2000* (New York: Random House, 1987); and also see Robert Gilpin, *War and Change in World Politics* (New York: Cambridge University Press, 1981).
23. Edward Friedman, "Chinese Nationalism, Taiwan Autonomy and the Prospects of a Larger War," *Journal of Contemporary China*, Vol. 6, No. 14, March 1997, pp. 5-32; also see, Barry Sautman, "Racial Nationalism and China's External Behaviour," *World Affairs*, Vol. 160, No. 2, Fall 1997, pp. 78-95; Downs and Saunders, n. 1.

24. For more details, see Chih-yu Shih, "Defining Japan: The Nationalist Assumption in China's Foreign Policy", *International Journal*, Vol. 50, No. 3, Summer 1995, pp. 539-563; and see Allen S. Whiting, *China Eyes Japan* (Berkeley, CA: University of California Press, 1989).
25. For related and more details, see Suisheng Zhao, "Chinese Intellectuals, Quest for Greatness," *China Quarterly*, No. 152, December 1997, pp. 725-745.
26. Song Qiang, *Zhang Zangzang and Qiao Bian, Zhongguo keyi shuo bu* [That China Can Still Say No] (Beijing: Zhonghua gongshang lianhe chubanshe, 1996); also see, Maria Hsia Chang and Xiaoyu Chen, "The Nationalist Ideology of the Chinese Military," *The Journal of Strategic Studies*, Vol. 21, No. 1, March 1998, pp. 44-64.
27. Wang Junyan, *Jingti Riben: zuori de qinlue yu jinri de kuozhang* (Hohehote: Inner Mongolia Press, 1996); cited in Deans, n. 17.
28. Guoming Yu and Xianyang Liu, *Zhongguo Minyi Yanjiu* (Research on Public Opinion in China) [Beijing: People's University Press, 1994] pp. 85-87; and Jie Chen, Yang Zhong, Ian Hillard and John Scheb, "Assessing Political Support in China: Citizen's Evaluations of Government Effectiveness and Legitimacy", *Journal of Contemporary China*, Vol. 6, No. 16, November 1997, p. 558.
29. Barry Sautman, "Sirens of the Strongman: Neo-Authoritarianism in Recent Chinese Political Theory", *China Quarterly*, No. 129, March 1992, pp. 72-102.
30. Yang Zhong, "Legitimacy Crisis and Legitimation in China", *Journal of Contemporary Asia*, Vol. 26, No. 2, 1996, pp. 212-218; also see, Downs et al., pp. 114-146.
31. Peter Hays Gries, *China's New Nationalism* (Los Angeles: University of California Press, 2004), p. 125.
32. Downs and Saunders., n. 1.
33. Takeuchi, n. 13, pp. 45-46.
34. Allen S. Whiting, "Chinese Nationalism and Foreign Policy After Deng", *The China Quarterly*, No. 142, June 1995, pp. 295-316.
35. Qiang, n. 26, pp. 80-83.

36. Chalmers Johnson, *Peasant Nationalism and Communist Power: The Emergence of Revolutionary China, 1937-1945* (Stanford, CA: Stanford University Press, 1962).
37. Michael J Green and Benjamin L Self, "Japan's Changing China Policy: From Commercial Liberalism to Reluctant Realism", *Survival*, Vol. 38, No. 2, Summer 1996, pp. 35-38.
38. Avery Goldstein, *Rising to the Challenge: China's Grand Strategy and International Security* (Stanford, California: Stanford University Press, 2005), p. 95.
39. For more and related information, see Chien-peng Chung, "The Diaoyu/Tiaoyutai/Senkaku Islands Dispute: Domestic Politics and the Limits of Diplomacy," *American Asian Review*, Vol. 16, No. 3, 1998, pp. 137.
40. Peter Gries, "China's 'New Thinking' on Japan", *The China Quarterly*, No. 184, December 2005.
41. Susan L. Shirk, *China: Fragile Superpower* (New York: Oxford University Press, 2007), p. 158, cited in Erik Beukel, "Popular Nationalism in China and the Sino-Japanese Relationship: The Conflict in the East China Sea," Report by the Danish Institute for International Studies, 2011.
42. Tu Weiming, "Cultural Identity and the Politics of Recognition in Contemporary Taiwan" in David Shambaugh, ed., *Contemporary Taiwan* (Oxford: Oxford University Press, 1998), pp. 71-96.
43. Deans, n. 17.
44. Ibid.
45. He, n. 8.
46. Youngnian Zheng, *Discovering Chinese Nationalism in China. Modernization, Identity, and International Relations* (Cambridge: Cambridge University Press, 1999).
47. Yinan He, "Remembering and Forgetting the War: Elite Mythmaking, Mass Reaction, and Sino-Japanese Relations, 1950-2006"*History & Memory: Studies in Representation of the Past*, Vol. 19, Fall/Winter 2007, pp. 51-56.
48. He, n. 21, pp. 6-7.
49. Beukel, n. 41.

50. Jian Yang, *China's Security Strategy Towards Japan: Perceptions, Policies and Prospects* (New Zealand: Centre for Strategic Studies, Victoria University of Wellington), No. 17, 2001, pp. 2-3.
51. Fu Xiao, *Sino-Japanese Relations: A Chinese Perspective* in Swanstrom et al., n. 13, p. 63.
52. Eugene A. Matthews, "Japan's New Nationalism: Armed and Dangerous?" *Foreign Affairs*, November/December 2003.
53. James J. Przystup, "Japan-China Relations: Not Quite All about Sovereignty – But Close", available at https://csis-prod.s3.amazonaws.com/s3fs-public/legacy_files/files/media/csis/pubs/0402qjapan_china.pdf
54. Daniel A. Métraux personally witnessed this incident and narrates it in his account, "The Senkaku Islands Dispute between China and Japan," *Southeast Review of Asian Studies*, Vol. 35, 2013, p. 220.
55. Edo Yusuke, *Senkaku Shima: do suru Nihon* (The Senkaku Islands: What Should Japan Do?) (Tokyo: Kotomo Shuppan, 1996).
56. "Governor Seen as Goading Administration into Action," *The Japan Times*, April 16, 2012.
57. "Tokyo Government in Talks with Owners to Buy Senkaku Islands: Ishihara," *Kyodo News*, April 15, 2012, available at http://english.kyodonews.jp/news/2012/04/153304.html
58. "*Senkaku konyu ni fumidashita,*" *The Asahi Shimbun*, September 26, 2012.
59. Report cited in *The Asahi Shimbun*, "Noda Government to buy Senkaku Islands for 2 Billion Yen", September 05, 2012.
60. "40% of Japan-China 40th Anniversary Events Cancelled Across Japan?" *The Japan Times*, September 30, 2012.
61. "China to Provide Weather Forecasts for Islands Claimed by Japan," *Bloomberg Report*, September 12, 2012, available at http://www.bloomberg.com/news/2012-09-12/china-to-provide-weather-forecasts-for-islands-claimed-byjapan.html
62. "Japanese Websites Come Under Attack as Senkaku Squabble Continues," *The Japan Times*, September 20, 2012.
63. "Protests Flare in China on Contentious Anniversary; The Pretext for Invasion 81 Years ago Fuels Rallies in 125 Cities," *The Japan*

Times, September 19, 2012, available at www.japantimes.co.jp/text/nn20120919a1.html

64. "82% Rap Lukewarm Response to Anti-Japan Protests in China over Senkakus: Mainichi Poll," *Mainichi,* October 01, 2012, available at http://mainichi.jp/english/english/newsselect/news/20121001p2a00m0na015000c.html
65. Statement by Akira Maeda, cited in Tomohiro Osaki, "Nationalism Rearing Ugly Head with Greater Frequency," *The Japan Times*, May 23, 2013.
66. Matthews, n. 52.
67. Ibid.
68. Craig Martin, "Reinterpreting Article 9 Endangers Japan's rule of Law," *The Japan Times*, June 27, 2014.
69. Reiji Yoshida, "Abe says Constitution Would Rule out Full-Scale Invasion, but 'Exceptions' are Unclear," *The Japan Times,* May 28, 2015.
70. Dennis McCornac, "New Nationalism in Japan," *The Diplomat*, August 21, 2014.
71. Karube Tadashi, "The Illusion of 'Rising Nationalism': Internationalism and Xenophobia in Today's Japan," *Nippon News*, July 14, 2014, Tokyo.
72. Quoted in Donald W. Jr Shriver, "The Long Road to Reconciliation: Some Moral Stepping Stones" in Robert L. Rothstein, ed., *After the Peace: Resistance and Reconciliation* (Boulder, CO: Lynne Rienner Publishers, 1999), p. 210.
73. World Bank Report, *Sharing Rising Incomes: Disparities in China*, (Washington DC: World Bank, 1997).

4. OIL, GAS, AND ECONOMICS OF THE CONFLICT

Conventional explanations alone cannot fully capture the dualistic nature of the dispute over the Senkaku/ Diaoyu Islands, given that several intertwined compulsions and motivations drive the debate. In this reference, economic interests constitute a vital part of the background for the conflicting jurisdictional claims.[1] While interdependence theories argue that economic interdependence and other transnational relations between countries lead to shared interests that will prevent military conflicts between two states,[2] perhaps, the most significant enquiry emerging from this bitter contest is whether the respective leaderships in Japan and China would continue pursuing economic sources of legitimacy even at a cost to their nationalist credentials? Is the complex partnership characterised as 'cold politics and hot economics' sustainable? A liberal peace perspective hinges upon an assumption that economic interdependence fosters peaceful relations by giving states an economic incentive to avoid costly military disputes.[3] The structure of Sino-Japanese economic interdependence deserves special attention, as it has undergone dramatic transformation. While rising interdependence provides greater economic incentives for both parties to avoid inflated conflict, increasing Japanese dependence on China puts forth a question about whether Japan's bargaining power vis-à-vis China would decline significantly, worsening the bilateral ties. Economic interdependence could be explosive, particularly if Chinese economic success allows Beijing to be more aggressive towards Japan, both economically, and strategically.[4] Beijing, has advocated that Tokyo has far more to lose in this contest. China's state-run and controlled publication, *People's Daily* argues that although the economic conflict would be a "double-edged sword," hurting China as well, "... if Japan continues its provocations, China will inevitably take on the fight."

Does Beijing currently have a clear strategic blueprint backed by economic designs, for the regional order in the coming decades? The concrete policy thinking coming out from Beijing and China's local provinces has *de facto* projected an image of China increasingly becoming the dominant power in East Asia, particularly in the economic arena.[5] The global implications of the dispute between China and Japan are underscored by the fact they compromise the world's second and third largest economies, respectively. The International Monetary Fund (IMF) updated its data in October 2014 on the global economy and, for the first time, ranked China's economy as the world's biggest, in terms of purchasing power parity. China and Japan account for nearly one-fifth of the global Gross Domestic Product (GDP) and their two-way trade amounts to over $ 340 billion a year. Moreover, the Centre for Economics and Business Research has forecast that by 2022, the Chinese economy, currently placed at the second spot, and at 53 per cent of the size of the US economy, will swell to 83 per cent of that size. Japan is expected to remain the world's third largest economy in 2022. Therefore, if relative power and economic dependence are the primary forces currently restraining the parties to the dispute, would their positions see a shift/alteration, once this power positioning strengthens in comparative terms of the military and economics? Chinese analyst Wu Di, among others, avers that Japan's economic situation is not viable in the long term. In 2011, debt-to-GDP ratio was greater than 200 per cent, while GDP was at the same level as it was in 2007. The savings of national companies, which have become less competitive internationally, largely underpins the country's fiscal deficit. Will they, at that point, be able to underwrite Japan's growing debt? Predicting that Japan will completely exhaust its national savings, so its national debt will represent 100 per cent of domestic savings, Wu claims that China's GDP will have overtaken that of the US and "Tokyo will be forced to ask for Beijing's financial assistance... China will be able to use its strong economic position to impose conditions, including a settlement on the Diaoyu Islands", terming that "sovereignty is a luxury" (主权是奢侈品 *zhuquan shi shechipin*).[6]

While politics has remained cold, to the extent of being frozen time and again, it is the economics that has somewhat salvaged a complete breakdown and fostered de-escalation of the Sino-Japanese conflict over territorial and maritime rights (*seirei keinetsu* in Japanese or *zhengleng jingre* in Chinese). The politico-economic interaction sometimes becomes perplexing. The post-war Sino-Japanese relationship is characterised by economic interdependence being confronted by political wariness and bitter contention. That the Diaoyu/Senkaku Islands have stretched to exacerbating global economic turmoil was signalled when, at the last minute, Chinese Central Bank Governor Zhou Xiaochuan and Finance Minister Xie Xuren, failed to show up at the IMF and World Bank annual meetings in Tokyo in October 2012. Many read this as a diplomatic snub by China to Japan.

The Turning Point

The status of the Senkaku Islands received little attention in the 1950s and 1960s. The turning point was the discovery of oil in the waters around the disputed islands in 1969. In fact, the future of offshore oil development is conceivably the most important driver behind the territorial dispute over the Senkaku Islands affecting 20,750 square nautical miles of marine space, and vast mineral resources in that area.[7] The scenario, however, changed permanently, when the Committee for Coordination of Joint Prospecting for Mineral Resources in Asian Offshore Areas (CCOP), under the auspices of the UN Economic Commission for Asia and the Far East (ECAFE) [presently known as the United Nations Economic and Social Commission for Asia and the Pacific (UNESCAP)] conducted extensive geophysical surveys in 1968 and 1969, and suggested the possible existence of the richest seabed with oil and hydrocarbon deposits in the waters off the Senkaku Islands. In May 1969, the committee declared that the continental shelf between Taiwan and Japan might be extremely rich in oil reserves, to the extent of being close to the Persian Gulf area.[8] The conclusions of the 1969 report on hydrocarbon reserves were later confirmed by independent Japanese as well as Chinese research. According to a 1994 estimate by the Japanese Ministry of the Economy, Trade and Industry Ministry (METI), deposits of oil and natural gas on the Japanese side of the East China Sea amounted to 500 million kilolitres in crude oil volume (according to a report cited in the *Yomiuri Shimbun*, August 28, 2004). And, the Chinese estimates of gas reserves in the East China Sea on the entire shelf ranged from 175-210 trillion cubic feet (in this reference, Saudi Arabia has proven gas reserves of 21.8 trillion cubic feet). Other estimates placed potential oil reserves on the shelf to be as high as 100 billion barrels (Saudi 261.7 billion barrels). More specifically, the US Energy Information Administration (EIA) reported China becoming the second largest net oil importer, behind the US in 2012, followed thereafter by Japan. Although foreign companies continue to be hesitant in investing, the EIA estimates the region in and around Senkaku to hold 60 to 100 million barrels of oil and 1 to 2 trillion cubic feet of natural gas – enough to provide energy sources to either state for 50-80 years.[9]

The Government of the PRC was confronted with serious problems regarding petroleum supply during the 1950s and 1960s. After the breakthrough discovery of several oil fields in northern China during the 1960s, China implemented a new, oil-oriented energy policy entitled "replacing coal by oil" (*yi you dai mei*) in order to reduce its coal-dominated energy consumption. Southeast China's coastal areas, particularly Shanghai municipality and Zhejiang province, are the most important industrial (and, thus, energy-consuming) bases having almost no hydrocarbon resources in their own territory. Consequently, the domestic oil/gas supply for these regions relies heavily on imports from the far northern and western provinces, thus, proving to be costly and insufficient. By contrast, the transportation of oil and gas from the East China Sea's continental shelf would be much easier and cheaper (given that it is located within 500 km approximately).[10]

The prospect of availability of large oil deposits moved China to declare the priority of its claims. In order to quell its growing demand for oil and gas, and to diversify away from its high dependence on supplies from West Asia, China started in the 1970s with prospecting and extraction of energy resources in the East China Sea. In December 2008, two Chinese patrol vessels of the China Marine Surveillance (CMS, *Haijiandui*) under the State Ocean Administration (SOA) entered territorial waters around the Senkaku Islands for the first time in an apparent move to strengthen the Chinese claim to the islands.[11] Meanwhile, Japan had reduced its oil dependence by one-third since the oil crises in the 1970s. Notwithstanding that, today, Japan is the world's largest Liquefied Natural Gas (LNG) importer (accounting for 40 percent of total world imports), second-largest coal importer, and third-largest net importer of crude oil and oil products.[12] While its energy consumption growth is expected to level off, Japan will continue importing vast quantities of oil and gas. According to the *World Energy Outlook* survey, released by the International Energy Agency, China's oil imports in 2030 are likely to reach about 500 million tonnes – the biggest in absolute terms of any country or region.

Fishing is a major interest for all the littoral states of the East China Sea. Japan and China signed a provisional fisheries agreement in November 1997, wherein it was agreed that a formal delimitation of the Exclusive Economic Zone (EEZ) would be deferred, joint management of the area between 30° 40' North and 27° North and beyond 52 nautical miles from the coasts of Japan and China would be provided, and traditional fishing activities would be continued in the vicinity of the disputed islands, with joint setting of fishing quotas for that area.[13] Although Japan and China concluded the 1997 fishery agreement effective from June 2000, it excluded from the application of the fisheries agreement the territorial waters adjacent to the Senkaku Islands. In 2012, a letter related to the

1997 Agreement about fishing in the EEZ was revealed in which Japanese Foreign Minister Obuchi conveyed to the Chinese Ambassador in Tokyo, Xu Duxin, that Japan's laws and regulations would not apply to the "waters in question" (*togai no suiiki*).[14] The Japanese government seems not to want to allow foreign fishermen uncontrolled access to the territorial waters around the Senkaku Islands, and has been patrolling the area, which has resulted in the expulsion of Chinese fishermen and subsequent protests by Taiwan and the PRC. Notably, Chinese fishing activity has increased vastly since then.[15]

UNCLOS and Economic Sovereignty

An arm of the Pacific Ocean bordering on the East Asian mainland, the East China Sea extends to the east of the chain of the Ryukyu Islands; northeast to Kyushu (the southernmost of Japan's main islands) and north to Cheju Island off the Korean peninsula; and hence west to China's eastern coast. On the south, the sea extends to the South China Sea through a shallow strait between Taiwan and mainland China. Whoever controls the Senkakus could claim economic and political sovereignty over a huge area of the East China Sea. The width of the East China Sea is 360 nautical miles which creates a problem for both China and Japan, since according to the United Nations Convention on the Law of Sea (UNCLOS), which both China and Japan have ratified, the EEZ extends 200 nautical miles from the baseline and within this area, the coastal nation has sovereign rights for the purpose of exploring all natural resources of the zone.[16] Chien-Peng Chung, an academic at the Department of Politics and Sociology of Lingnan University, Hong Kong, maintains that there is still no clarity on whether the islands may be used to claim fishing and petroleum rights in the adjacent waters. This argument is attributed to Article 121(3) of the Law of the Sea, which states that "rocks, which cannot sustain human inhabitation or economic life of their own shall have no EEZ."[17] China, however, argues that the natural extension of its continental shelf, which runs right up to the Okinawa trough, should be used to determine each state's EEZ. This proposal is undoubtedly unacceptable to Japan because it would bring Chinese territorial waters in propinquity with Okinawa.[18]

Fig 4.1: Exclusive Economic Zones (EEZs) in the East China Sea

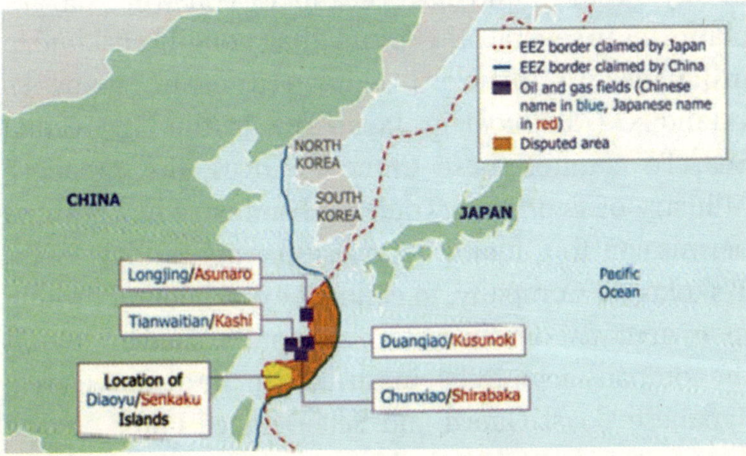

Source: As cited in the US Energy Information Administration (EIA) Monitor, October 05, 2012.

Guo Rongxing, head of the Regional Economics Committee of the Regional Science Association of China, Peking University, states that under UNCLOS, China has the right to claim a continental shelf as far as 350 nautical miles. However, Japan also has the right to an EEZ extending 200 nautical miles from its shore. Since China's coast is within 400 nautical miles of the nearest undisputed Japanese island, China's and Japan's claimed EEZs overlap in the East China Sea.[19] China is developing many oil/gas fields just to the west of what Japan claims is the median line separating the two countries' EEZs. This has caused apprehension in the Japanese government, as it believes that China may be exploiting gas reserves located on the Japanese side.[20] China's state-owned oil companies have been producing oil and gas in three fields – namely, Pinghu, Chunxiao (*Shirakaba* in Japanese), and Tianwaitian (*Kashiide* in Japanese) – and have begun to construct oil/gas platforms in several others, including Longjing (*Asunaro* in Japanese), Canxue or Lengquan (*Kikyo* in Japanese), Duanqiao (*Kusunoki* in Japanese), in the East China Sea. To counter these Chinese moves, the Japanese Ministry of Economy, Trade and Industry has granted permission to a major Japanese private oil developer, Teikoku Oil Company, to conduct experimental drilling in an area just on the eastern side of the median line. If the company actually begins drilling in the disputed area, Japanese Coast Guard and Self-Defence Force escorts may be needed for security reasons since the Chinese Navy would probably approach this area as well.[21]

In May 2004, the conflict flared up when the Japanese maritime authorities detected a Chinese maritime research ship operating in what Japan considers its own EEZ in the East China Sea. Japan's request to end the survey activities notwithstanding, China began the construction of a natural gas drilling facility. In response, Japan launched a survey of the disputed area and started exploring for natural gas.[22] This was confronted with a series of Chinese demonstrations outside the Japanese Embassy in Beijing protesting Japan's 'illegal' oil exploration activities (*Kyodo News* 2004). For many commentators, the summer of 2004 marked one of the lowest points in Sino-Japanese relations in the post-normalisation era.[23] From 2004 to 2008, China and Japan held a series of high-level meetings to address their growing maritime boundary disputes and joint/cooperative development of the hydrocarbon resources in the disputed area. Although there has been minimal progress towards joint/cooperative development, on June 18, 2008, following 12 rounds of talks, Beijing and Tokyo reached an agreement on:

- The joint development of a zone straddling both sides of the median line proposed by Japan, including the oil/gas field called "Longjing" by China (*Asunaro* in Japanese)
- Japan's participation in China's Chunxiao gas field (*Shirakaba* in Japanese)[24]

It needs to be highlighted that the most important hydrocarbon resource in the East China Sea is gas.

Although gas has a share of only about 3 per cent in China's total energy consumption, it is rising fast, driven by a deliberate policy of the Chinese government to reduce polluting fossil fuel – i.e., environmentally damaging high coal consumption. Notably, China is by far the world's largest producer and consumer of coal, accounting for 46 per cent of global coal production and 49 per cent of global coal consumption – almost as much as the rest of the world combined. As a manufacturing country that has large electric power requirements, China's coal consumption fuels its economic growth.[25] Meanwhile, gas seems to be a slightly more delicate issue, as China has been producing it from a field in a disputed part of the East China Sea, claiming it to be within its EEZ. Japan protested against this unilateral move in 2009 and in stronger language in July 2013, since the two countries had agreed in 2008 to explore gas resources together and halt development in contested areas. A US Congressional Research Service report confirms that this agreement has not been implemented. Although Taiwan has not actively pursued such resources in the East China Sea on its own, its National Oil Corporation has entered into a joint venture with the Chinese undertaking. Furthermore, in 2007, despite its own growing gas production, China started to import gas in the form of LNG. There is a growing sense in Beijing that control of oil and gas fields is very important for guaranteeing a stable supply, rather than relying on market forces and diversification, as Japan does. It is well known that this Chinese approach is attracting considerable international criticism about its impact on certain conflict zones (for instance, Darfur in Sudan).[26] While the Japanese government had attempted to placate the Chinese by abstaining from even surveying the hydrocarbon resources in the disputed area, this holding tactic became unsustainable in the face of China's relentless exploration of the area, to the point of now extracting gas and oil in the immediate vicinity of Japan's proposed maritime border. The unequal distribution of the economic stakes (i.e. China's advance in exploiting the hydrocarbons of the East China Sea) is a necessary pre-condition to concluding an economic interest-based agreement.

Clearly, the presence of considerable oil and gas resources, discovered ever since the 1969 report came out, casts a direct implication on reduction of dependence on imports from West Asia, and goaded China to press for its territorial claims, including the whole continental shelf up to the Okinawa trough for the delimitation of the EEZ. Implicitly, driving the argument that as the bigger country with a greater need for energy resources, China's claims to these resources are far more weighty and legitimate. This is similar to China's official insistence that its continental shelf demand is in accordance with UNCLOS, because of the length of its coastal line and its population there, in contrast to the narrow and sparsely populated Okinawa Island chain. Chinese Ambassador Wang Jin, echoed this stance in Tokyo in 2005 when he stated, "In contrast to the long coastline of China, Japan consists of a chain of islands. Seen from this special geographical point of view, the median line as the border between the two countries does not agree with the principle of equity."[27]

China has recently become the world's largest global energy consumer. With gas imports rising and China becoming a net natural gas importer for the first time in almost two decades in 2007, the US Energy Administration forecasts that China's oil and natural gas consumption will continue to increase in the coming years, putting additional pressure on the Chinese government to seek out new supplies to meet domestic demand. And these statistics are resonant with Japan too, being the third largest net importer of crude oil and the world's largest importer of LNG, owing to few domestic energy resources. This only makes it palpable that both Tokyo and Beijing have immense stakes in extracting hydrocarbon resources from the East China Sea to help meet their respective domestic demands.[28]

While beginning exploration activities in the East China Sea in the 1980s, China discovered the Pinghu oil and gas field in 1983. Japan co-financed two oil and gas pipelines running from the Pinghu field to Shanghai and the Ningbo onshore terminal on the Chinese mainland through the Asian Development Bank (ADB)and its own Japanese Bank of International Cooperation (JBIC). More recently, both China and Japan have concentrated their oil and gas extraction efforts in the contested Xihu/Okinawa trough. Most fields are operated as joint ventures between the Chinese National Offshore Oil Corporation (CNOOC) and the China Petroleum & Chemical Corporation (Sinopec) with support from foreign firms and other partners, such as the Shanghai government. CNOOC listed its East China Sea proved oil reserves at 18 million barrels in 2011, according to an annual report, while the other partners have not publicly released their reserves figures.[29] Only the Pinghu field, operational since 1998, has produced oil in significant quantities to date. Pinghu's production peaked at around 8,000 to 10,000 barrels per day (bbl/d) of oil and condensate in the late 1990s, and levelled off to around 400 bbl/d in recent years. In the medium-term, the East China Sea is not expected to become a significant supplier of oil.[30]

Significantly, the EIA estimates that the East China Sea has between 1 and 2 trillion cubic feet (Tcf) in proven and probable natural gas reserves. The region may also have significant upside potential in terms of natural gas. Chinese sources point to as much as 250 Tcf in undiscovered gas resources, mostly in the Xihu/Okinawa trough. CNOOC listed its East China Sea proved gas reserves at 300 billion cubic feet (Bcf) in 2011, according to an annual report. In 2012, an independent evaluation estimated probable reserves of 119 Bcf of natural gas in LS 36-1, a promising gas field north of Taiwan, currently being developed as a joint venture between CNOOC and the UK firm Primeline Petroleum Corp. The uncontested Pinghu field began production in 1998, reaching a peak of approximately

40 to 60 million cubic feet per day (Mmcf/d) in the mid-2000s, however declining in recent years. Chinese companies discovered a large oil and gas field group in 1995 in the Xihu/Okinawa trough. Chunxiao/Shirabaka is the largest gas field in this group and is used on occasion to reference all fields in the area. China began producing at the contested Tianwaitian/Kashi field in 2006, claiming it as part of its Exclusive Economic Zone. According to industry sources, Tianwaitian/Kashi produced between 10 and 18 Mmcf/d in the past several years.

China has not released any production data from the Chunxiao/Shirabaka field, citing concerns about the regional dispute. The Chinese government prioritises boosting the share of natural gas as part of total energy consumption to alleviate high pollution from the country's heavy coal use. To that end, Chinese authorities intend to ramp up production and increase East China Sea gas flow into the Yangtze river delta region, which includes Shanghai and Hangzhou, two large cities with a growing gas demand. According to an industry source, gas from the East China Sea supplied approximately 12 percent of the natural gas needs of Zhejiang province in the first half of 2012, though natural gas remains a small part of the region's total energy mix.[31]

Pure economic and logistical reasons make the oil and gas reserves in the East China Sea more useful for China than for Japan. In the case of gas, which seems to be most abundant in the contested area, it is important to note that Japan imports gas only in the form of LNG and, therefore, a big land-based gasefication plant would have to be built. This would require laying a pipeline, which would be uneconomical because it would have to lead to Japan's major consumer centres, over 2,000 km from the gas fields. Moreover, such a pipeline would have to cross deep waters, including the Okinawa trough.[32] On the other hand, in the case of oil, opinions appear to be far more diverse because extracted oil can more easily be loaded on tankers, although using the existing Chinese pipeline structure to the Chinese mainland would be cheaper.[33] Evidently, these economic and logistical circumstances have no impact on legal circumstances and do not provide ground for demanding that Japan should abandon its territorial claims to facilitate a solution. There are no practical obstacles to Japan taking part in the exploitation of the oil and gas fields, as well as sharing the profits as part of a bilateral agreement.[34]

Economic Fallout of the Dispute

The print and electronic forms of media in Japan refer to three kinds of China 'threat': (1) China's remarkable economic development; (2) China becoming the factory of the world; and (3) growing imports from China hollowing out the Japanese industry. Beijing is not only a large exporter but also a large importer with roughly equal volumes of exports and imports.[35] The acceleration in the number of Japanese companies setting up business in the Chinese market, the expansion of Chinese domestic demand, and other factors, have caused Japan's dependence on trade with China to drift upwards. This new development has both positive and negative implications.

Bilateral economic friction in the 1980s demonstrated the aggravating effect of popular nationalism on the Sino-Japanese political conflict. Economic problems between the two countries were usually caused by factors on both sides. For instance, China's trade deficit with Japan in the 1980s was rooted in the structural difference between the two economies, Japan's general trade barriers, China's overheated demands for foreign products, and its lack of quality control, and orderly distribution and service systems. Similarly, the causes of stagnating Japanese technology transfer and capital investment to China before the 1990s were manifold. However, the Chinese tended to blame the Japanese side for all these problems, with the exception of only a few economic experts who would admit some degree of Chinese responsibility as well. Such an obvious bias could not be understood as simply a negotiation tactic because not just high-ranking Chinese officials directly involved in economic negotiations with Japan, but also, ordinary Chinese shared this view. Behind the bias was the Chinese sense of historical entitlement with regards to Japan. It was taken for granted that Japan should generously assist China's modernisation and attend to all its economic needs, for Japan's past aggression had inflicted devastating pain on China. Therefore, when China's trade deficit with Japan peaked in the mid-

1980s, Chinese students instantly linked the economic issue with history. They saw the flooding of Japanese goods into the Chinese market as Japan's renewed attempt at 'economic invasion', and accused it of holding back China's technological development. One of their demands was to boycott imported Japanese goods (*rihuo*), an act to emulate the anti-Japanese mass movement of the 1930s. In the *China Youth Daily* poll of 1996, 96.3 percent of respondents believed that Japanese investment in China was to occupy the market and seek profit, 50.7 percent thought it was to control China economically, and 45.3 percent thought it was to dump outmoded facilities, with only 9.5 percent believing it was to help Chinese economic development.[36] While China can make use of, and learn from, Japan's industrial technologies and experience to speed up its modernisation drive, Japan, on the other hand, can make use of China's advantages in labour, energy and land, and rejuvenate its own economy by benefitting from the Chinese economic growth.[37] The combined GDP of China and Japan accounts for about 80 percent of the East Asian total; their population, 70 percent of East Asia's; and their import and export trade volumes, 60 percent of those of the region. Against the backdrop of economic globalisation, the bilateral economic interaction has been interwoven with the global and regional economies.[38]

However, the flare-up of the dispute over the Senkakus seems to have only prolonged the Japanese recession. Chinese consumers staged boycotts of

Japanese products, sales of Japanese automobiles in China are yet to recover, Chinese factories began sourcing products from South Korean component suppliers over the Japanese, and the US displaced China as Japan's largest export market. The contest has also contributed to a decline in Japan's shipments to China and Tokyo's industrial output falling 1.7 percent – the lowest since the aftermath of the 2011 earthquake.[39] The greatest fallout of the Senkaku crisis came in the form of damage to Japanese economic activities, caused by a partial consumer boycott, notably the fall of car sales in China and that of Chinese tourism to Japan. Adding to the woes, the Chinese Communist Party has stoked nationalist sentiment under the reactionary slogan of "boycotting Japanese goods," with middle class consumers joining campaigns against buying Japanese-made cars or taking holidays in Japan. It has been estimated that since 2012, Chinese tourist numbers to Japan could have fallen by about 70 percent, while Japanese tourists to China decreased by 30 percent. With as many as 46,000 seat cancellations, Japan's largest airline, Nippon Airways Co., faced heavy losses between September and November 2012 owing to the row over the Senkakus – cutting sales by almost 10 billion Japanese yen. Overall, bilateral trade decreased by 3.9 percent in 2012 to $329 billion, the first drop since the collapse of the Lehman Investment Bank in 2009.[40] Moreover, fearing attacks from anti-Japan protesters, Fast Retailing Co., the seller of the very popular *UNIQLO* casual wear brand, temporarily shut nearly 60 of its 169 stores in China for almost a fortnight, according to Yukie Sakaguchi. Stores and supermarkets near the Japanese Embassy in Beijing, Hunan province, Shiga prefecture, central Japan, incurred losses of almost 500 million yen. China accounts for 19.7 percent of Japanese exports, compared to 15.3 percent for the US and it has often been reported that Chinese customs officials are known to deliberately delay Japanese imports.

Notably, JP Morgan Chase projected that Japanese car exports to China would crash by 70 percent in the final quarter of 2012, with auto parts and other goods, like electronics, down by 40 percent. In fact, the worst hit sector remains automobiles, with leading Japanese maker Toyota Motor Corp., Japan's biggest car-maker, selling 840,500 vehicles in China in 2012, the first annual drop since 2002, finally announcing that its output in China fell the most in at least a decade. Following this, Nissan experienced a 24 percent drop in the December 2012 China sales, and Honda a 19 percent fall.[41] In November 2012, it was announced that, compared with the previous year, Toyota's production in China fell by 61.1 per cent, Nissan's by 44 percent, Honda's by 54.2 percent and Mitsubishi Motors' by 84.6 percent.[42] This had a strong effect on the individual car-makers, given that China accounts for 25 percent of Nissan's net profit, 21 percent of Toyota's and 16 percent of Honda's.[43]

According to June Teufel Dreyer, a specialist in Chinese politics at the Miami University, Florida,

"China will continue to push its claims to sovereignty until Beijing gets what it wants." Terming the given setting over the Senkaku Islands a "match made in heaven", Jesper Koll, head of equity research at JP Morgan in Tokyo, says, "Japan has intellectual property, brands and capital, while China has people, markets and purchasing power." In what can be termed as a pragmatic opinion, Liu Li-Gang, chief economist for Greater China at the Australia and New Zealand Banking Group Ltd., who previously also worked for the World Bank, articulates that "... both economies will lose in the end... Japan will lose a big market and China will not be able to leverage on Japan's technology and investment for growth." For Japan, it would be very difficult to accept the emergence of a Sino-centric order. For China, the current regional order that largely hinges on the Japan-US alliance is not desirable. In an interview to *The Washington Post* in November 2014, Japanese Prime Minister Shinzo Abe underlined his administration's primary objective – to lift the Japanese economy out of deflation (which has continued for the past 15 years), aiming at simultaneously attaining economic revitalisation and fiscal consolidation. Many Chinese observers increasingly believe that Japan's economic well-being has to depend on the Chinese market. They believe that economic symbiosis is increasingly becoming asymmetric in China's favour. Coupled with the growing perception in China that Japan is stuck in a long-term economic stagnation and slowdown, this may lead to the possibility of China using some economic leverage to put pressure on Japan on political and security matters. China's handling of the Diaoyu/Senkaku dispute in September 2010 was perhaps an illustration of things moving towards that direction.[44]

Territorial disputes are best approached eclectically, through a structured framework that is viable as it studies the impact of military technological growth on willingness and opportunity, a conception of contiguity that reflects maritime territory, and the impact of regime type on state willingness to pursue military means of resolution. States more likely to adopt aggressive, military-oriented foreign policy practices, when faced with real or perceived threats to territory, are put through the litmus test of the web of economic symbiosis – as amply demonstrated in the case of the Senkaku Islands.

Notes

1. Jean-Marc F. Blanchard, "China's Peaceful Rise and Sino-Japanese Territorial and Maritime Tensions" in Sujian Guo, ed., *China's "Peaceful Rise" in the 21st Century: Domestic and International Conditions* (Ashgate: Publisher Aldershot, 2006), pp. 225-231; also see John Donaldson and Alison Williams, "Understanding Maritime Jurisdictional Disputes: The East China Sea and Beyond," *Journal of International Affairs*, Vol. 59, No. 1, Fall/Winter 2005, pp. 135-156.
2. For more on the subject, see Robert O Keohane and Joseph S Nye, *Power and Interdependence* (New York: Longman, 2001).
3. Min Gyo Koo, "The Senkaku/Diaoyu Dispute and Sino-Japanese Political-Economic Relations: Cold Politics and Hot Economics?" *The Pacific Review*, Vol. 22, No. 2, May 2009, pp. 205-232.
4. Ibid.

5. Ming Wan, "The Great Recession and China's Policy toward Asian Regionalism," *Asian Survey*, Vol. 50, No. 3, May/June 2010, pp. 521-530.
6. Wu Di, "The Diaoyu Islands Crisis and the Strategy of 'Hiding one's Talents and Biding one's Time'", *Lianhe Zaobao,* September 15, 2012.
7. For more details, see Martin A. Pratt, et al., *Jane's Exclusive Economic Zones 1999-2000*; also see Seokwoo Lee, "The 1951 San Francisco Peace Treaty with Japan and the Territorial Disputes in East Asia," *Pacific Rim Law and Policy Journal*, Vol. 11, No. 1, 2002, pp. 87-88.
8. Zhiguo Gao and Wu Jilu, "Key Issues in the East China Sea: A Status Report and Recommended Approaches" in Selig Harrison, ed., *Seabed Petroleum in Northeast Asia: Conflict or Cooperation?*(Washington D.C., Woodrow Wilson International Center for Scholars, 2005), p. 32; also see, *Report of the Sixth Session of the Committee for Co-ordination of Joint Prospecting for Mineral Resources in Asian Offshore Areas,* U.N. Doc. E/CN.1 l/L.239 (1970), pp. 51-67.
9. For details, see J. Curtin, "Stakes Rise in Japan, China Gas Dispute," *Asia Times*, October 19, 2005; also see, Lee Jae-Hyung, "China's Expanding Maritime Ambitions in the Western Pacific and the Indian Ocean," *Contemporary Southeast Asia,* Vol. 24, No. 3, 2002, pp. 549-568.
10. Guo Rongxing, "Territorial Disputes and Seabed Petroleum Exploitation: Some Options for the East China Sea," Center for Northeast Asian Policy Studies, The Brookings Institution, Washington D.C., September 2010.
11. Yoshikazu Shimizu, "*Kan Seiken ga minogashita Chugoku 'goki no naka no morosa*'", *Chuo Koron,* November 2010, p. 65.
12. The US Energy Information Administration (EIA), *Analysis Brief*, 'Japan', January 30, 2015.
13. Agreement on Fisheries (China-Japan) *Reprinted in Japanese Annual International Law*, No. 122, 1998.
14. For more details, see Reinhard Drifte, "The Senkaku/Diaoyu Islands Territorial Dispute between Japan and China: Between the

Materialization of the "China Threat" and Japan "Reversing the Outcome of World War II"? *UNISCI Discussion Papers*, No. 32, May 2013, p. 24.

15. Yves Tiberghien, "The Diaoyu/Senkaku Dispute: Analyzing the Chinese Perspective," *Canada-Asia Agenda*, No. 30, October 2012, available at http://www.asiapacific.ca/sites/default/files/canada-asia_agenda_30_v11.pdf]
16. United Nations, *United Nations Convention on the Law of Sea 1982*, available at http://www.un.org/Depts/los/convention_agreements/texts/unclos/closindx.htm; also see Erica S Downs and Phillip C Saunders, "Legitimacy and the Limits of Nationalism: China and the Diaoyu Islands," *International Security*, Vol. 23, No. 3, Winter 1998/99, pp. 114-146.
17. Chien-Peng Chung, "Resolving China's Island Disputes: A Two-Level Game Analysis," *Journal of Chinese Political Science*, Vol. 12, No. 1, 2007.
18. For more details, see Sheila A Smith, "Japan and the East China Sea Dispute," *Orbis*, Vol. 56, No. 3, Summer 2012, pp. 370-390.
19. Rongxing, n. 10.
20. For more, see "Oil and Gas in Troubled Waters," *The Economist*, Vol. 377, No. 8447, October 8, 2005, p. 72.
21. Rongxing, n. 10.
22. For more details, see JJ Pryzstup, "Not the Best of Times," *Comparative Connections*, Vol. 6, No. 3, 2004, pp. 117-128.
23. Interview conducted by Min Gyo Koo with Japan's Ministry of Foreign Affairs officials in Tokyo in June 2004, cited in Koo, n. 3.
24. Rongxing, n. 10.
25. "China Produces and Consumes Almost as Much Coal as the Rest of the World Combined," US Energy Information Administration, *Analysis Brief*, May 14, 2014.
26. Reinhard Drifte, "Japanese-Chinese Territorial Disputes in the East China Sea – Between Military Confrontation and Economic cooperation," Paper for the Asia Research Centre, London School of Economics and Political Science, August 2008.
27. Kyoko Hamakawa and Higashi Shinakai, "*ni okeru Nitchu kyoukai*

gakutei mondai Kokkai Tsoshokan," *Issue Brief*, No. 547, June 16, 2006, p. 3, available at http://210.128.252.171/jp/data/publication/issue/0547.pdf cited in Ibid.

28. *East China Sea*, US Energy Information Administration, September 25, 2012, p. 2.
29. Ibid.
30. Ibid.
31. Ibid., p. 3; the data has also been collated from sources, including reports by the Chinese National Offshore Oil Corporation, *IHS Global Insight*, and *Japan Economic Newswire*.
32. Yasuhiro Goto, *Kokusai Mondai*, April 2005, p. 38; also see Dai Tan, "The Diaoyu/Senkaku Dispute: Bridging the Cold Divide," *Santa Clara Journal of International Law*, Vol. 5, No. 1, 2006 pp. 134-168.
33. Drifte, n. 26.
34. Ibid.
35. Ye Zicheng, *Inside China's Grand Strategy: The Perspective from the People's Republic*, Translated by Steven I Levine and Gouoli Liu, (New Delhi: KW Publishers Pvt Ltd, 2013), p. 144.
36. For more details, see *China Youth Daily*, February 15, 1997.
37. J Zhang, *The 30th Anniversary of China-Japan Relations: Economy (1978-2008)* (Beijing: China Social Science Academic Press, 2008).
38. Fu Xiao, "Sino-Japanese Relations: A Chinese Perspective," in Niklas Swanstrom and Ryosei Kokubun, eds., *Sino-Japanese Relations: Rivals or Partners in Regional Cooperation?* (Singapore: World Scientific Publishing Co. Ltd., 2013).
39. "China-Japan Dispute Takes Rising Toll on Top Asian Economies," *Bloomberg News*, January 9, 2013.
40. "Trade with China Falls First Time in Three Years," *The Japan Times*, January 11, 2013.
41. "Toyota Delays Plan for China Expansion," *The Japan Times*, January 09, 2013.
42. "Japan Car Production in China Down 49 Percent in October," *NHK*, November 29, 2012.
43. "Factory Shift to non-Chinese Sites Seen Accelerating; Companies

Reopen as Anger Eases in China," *The Japan Times,* September 22, 2012.

44. Li Mingjiang, "China and Japan: Hot Economics, Cold Politics", in Purnendra Jain and Lam Peng Er, eds., *Japan's Strategic Challenges in a Changing Regional Environment* (MA: World Scientific Publishing Co. Pvt. Ltd., 2013), p. 59.

5. THE CHINA-JAPAN-AMERICA TRIANGLE: COERCIVE DIPLOMACY, MILITARY SUPREMACY, AND STRATEGIC POWER INTERPLAY

The "China as a threat" view and the "declinist" theory that see China's path-breaking economic growth as eclipsing the status of Japan as the economic superpower, have tended to conflate the strategic debate in Japan, paving the way for a clamour to confront a militarily expansionist China (*gunkaku chugoku to no taiketsu*).[1] In this reference, from the power-transition theory perspective, the determination of Sino-Japanese relations is a necessary consequence of the 'rise of China'. Japan's defensive response to the rise of China might be taken as offensive by China, which, in turn, would make Sino-Japanese relations even more tense. The negative spirals of tension caused by defensive strategies taken as offensive is termed a security dilemma, which might occur because "in an uncertain and anarchic international system, mistrust between two or more potential adversaries can lead each side to take precautionary and defensively motivated measures that are perceived as offensive threats".[2] By issuing 'coercive action' on Japan in the dispute over the Senkakus, China is visibly using the dual strategy of *issue linkage* and *coercive diplomacy*. Japanese security specialists speak of China's "deception diplomacy" and warn that China is simply biding its time until its force modernisation is complete. Issue linkage occurs when a state deliberately links two or more distinct foreign policy issues together, claiming that resolution of one issue cannot occur without resolution of the other. Meanwhile, coercive diplomacy is an attempt by one state to compel another state through some type of coercion, threat, or use of force, to reconsider or shift its foreign policy on a certain issue. The logic of coercive diplomacy is to back up a demand with a threat of punishment/punitive action that is credible and strong enough to persuade the adversary to comply with the demand. By combining these two foreign policy strategies, when crises arise, either deliberately or accidentally, China uses threats in the territorial dispute as bargaining leverage to compel Japan to shift its policy on another issue such as economic aid, Japan-US security agreements, or potential Japanese troop deployments.[3]

China has been able to take advantage of the endurance of its territorial dispute with Japan and use it as bargaining leverage to achieve shifts in Japanese foreign policies regarding other disputed issues that it otherwise would not be able to influence – thereby hoping that threats will persuade Japan to seriously reconsider its position on certain policies or actions. A state using the strategy of coercive diplomacy (coercer) threatens an adversary in order to get the adversary to halt an action it initiated. Coercive diplomacy is not a traditional military strategy, but a political strategy that uses just enough of a threat to credibly demonstrate its resolve and achieve the set objectives.[4] The primary objective of coercive diplomacy is to "create in the opponent, the expectation of costs of sufficient magnitude to erode his motivation to continue doing what he is doing."[5] In territorial disputes, coercive diplomacy is sometimes used to persuade the adversary to halt some action it is undertaking with regard to the actual disputed territory.

Issue linkage occurs when a state making territorial claims strategically links territorial threats to other, initially unrelated, foreign policy issues, making the explicit or implicit claim that resolving one issue will affect, or be affected by, the resolution of another disputed issue. With strategic issue linkage, states can use one issue where they have bargaining leverage in order to persuade adversaries to make a change in an issue area where they have relatively weaker bargaining leverage. In some cases, strong states will use issue linkage to extend their relative power from one issue area to another, while, in other cases, weak states can use issue linkage in an attempt to prevent another state from exercising its power.[6] China knows that it has less economic leverage when it comes to influencing

Japanese decisions about aid and investment in particular. However, China also knows it has more bargaining leverage by using threats of military force. By shifting the military leverage into an economic issue area, China links the two issues together so it can influence an economic issue using military leverage. A state using an issue as positive leverage, also known as the "carrot" approach in diplomacy, offers rewards in one issue area if the adversary changes its approach in another issue area. The strategy to achieve negative leverage through a threat, also known as the "stick" approach in diplomacy, is used just as frequently. The current on-going development of natural gas resources in the East China Sea is only a small part of the anticipated oil and gas resources, which cannot be exploited until the dispute is fully settled. China will inevitably continue to claim that its EEZ extends to the continental shelf, while Japan will continue to claim the median line between the two states to determine each state's EEZ zones. The islands' dispute is critical in determining rights to EEZ zones and, therefore, oil and gas resources, as well as fishing and other maritime resources.[7]

Sovereignty Game Framework

The Chinese and Japanese views towards each other have been compounded by an amalgam of daunting challenges, including historical baggage, unremitting strategic distrust, unmistakable clashes of national interests, and even vaguely defined social stereotypes.[8]

These inherent misgivings about each other have convoluted the politico-military narrative in Beijing and Tokyo. And this, consequently, impacts upon the foundational premise of the debate on the sovereignty claims. The resources at the disposal of the state to stake sovereignty can be diversified into three kinds: (1) economic; (2) political; and (3) military, which involve threat or use of force, balancing through alliances, and/or the development of capabilities.

Meanwhile, in addition to the resources, the symbolic value signifying the importance of the territory in question in terms of nationalism and national identity also plays a vital part in the corresponding approach taken by the involved parties in the contest. Japan's maintaining a "hands off" approach throughout the 1990s, led Tokyo to lose ground in the sovereignty game, while enabling China to assert its sovereignty claims over the Diaoyu and improve its position on sovereignty. In 1978, a right-wing Japanese group built a lighthouse on one of the islands, to be partially restored during the 1980s. The Maritime Self-Defence Forces (MSDF) issued a report that stated they would soon approve the authorisation for a new lighthouse to be placed on the Senkaku Islands. The immediate spark of the 1996 crisis was when the Japan Youth Federation (JYF) built a 5-metre high aluminium lighthouse on the privately owned island of Kitakojima. The JYF submitted an application to the MSDF to consider making the lighthouse 'official'. China's *Sing Tao* newspaper reported that the islands were under surveillance by more than 10 PRC naval vessels and that the People's Liberation Army Air Force (PLAAF) had sent several planes over the islands. On September 24, Japanese Foreign Minister Yukihiko Ikeda informed his PRC counterpart Qian Qichen that there were no plans to officially recognise the lighthouse. The 1996 lighthouse incident represented a major foreign policy success for Japan, with Japan emerging with effective control and reiterating the "no dispute exists" position.

Chinese analysts state that while entering the 21st century, China's views of the US-Japan alliance were conditioned by two new governments in both Washington and Tokyo. The Bush administration initially changed the focus of its East Asia strategy. Enhancing the strategic role of Japan in East Asia became a priority of President's Bush policy. Japanese Prime Minister Junichiro Koizumi's visits to the Yakusuni Shrine amid Beijing's repeated protests strained Sino-Japanese relations very badly. China was convinced that Japan's grand strategy was already set—to ally with the US to hedge against China's rise in East Asia.[9] Beijing already noticed the Bush administration's East Asia strategy of "uplifting Japan and downgrading China" that made the overall Japanese foreign policy more assertive, particularly in military and security affairs, including its increasingly proactive role in the security alliance and related stand on Taiwan; its more provocative policy toward the 'Diaoyu' Islands; and finally, what some perceived as Japan's increasing intransigence in acknowledging its history of aggression in the region.[10] In fact, it can be argued that from the administration of Junichirō Koizumi on, there was a perceptible shift in the dynamics of the sovereignty game, in that it improved Japan's position on the issue, however, it came at the cost of a deep-freeze in bilateral ties (2001-06) attributed, among other reasons, to Koizumi's visits to the Yasukuni Shrine.

When Prime Minister Yukio Hatoyama and the Democratic Party of Japan (DPJ) Secretary-General Ichiro Ozawa took over power in August 2009, they unveiled a vision for creating an "equal alliance" with the US and a more "autonomous foreign policy" that emphasised improving relations with Asia, especially China.[11] This pronouncement stretched to the extent that Hatoyama called for an "equal alliance" and an "East Asian Community" which excluded the US. Often termed as Hatoyama's "naïve" foreign policy, it caused considerable damage to the credibility of the US-Japan alliance, and likely bolstered Chinese assertiveness. Apparently, this is one reason why former US Secretary of State Hillary Clinton felt compelled to reaffirm American interests in the freedom of navigation in the South China Sea, and the US treaty obligation to Japan in regard to the Senkakus.[12] While meeting with then Chinese President Hu Jintao at the UN in September 2009, Prime Minister Hatoyama declared his desire to turn the East China Sea into a "sea of fraternity instead of a sea of disputes".[13] For that matter, the Hatoyama administration made conscious efforts to modify the Liberal Democratic Party's pro-American foreign policy by rebalancing its relations with the US (calling for more equal bilateral ties), on the one hand, and better ties with its Asian neighbours (including China), on the other. But Hatoyama's campaign promise to relocate the Futenma US Marine Corps Air Station in Okinawa proved untenable. Moreover, his desire for a more even relationship with both the US and China strained ties with the former, whose security alliance with Japan is traditionally seen as a main tenet of regional security. One Chinese scholar concluded that the DPJ government began to seriously give up its thinking of relying upon the US to deal with China.[14] Chinese scholars came to the conclusion that "only when Japan is serious about returning to Asia, could it meaningfully join the process of East Asia integration."[15] The Chinese argument is that "Tokyo has to resolve its problem of 'strategic unclearness' in its East Asia policy."[16]

However, there was growing disappointment with traditional politics and frustration with the failure to restore Japan to a prosperous path. This environment gave rise to populist and nationalist politicians who were seen as credible alternatives to ineffectual and ambiguous leaders. Former Tokyo Governor Ishihara and Osaka Mayor Toru Hashimoto have driven these movements, in part. A Japanese analyst wrote that the Japanese wanted to "stop floating like a ghost in the sea of perpetual apologies for the Asia-Pacific War of 70 years ago".[17] Ishihara captured popular opinion after the 2010 boat incident and forced the government's hand over the Senkaku Island purchase.[18] Prime Minister

Shinzo Abe who took over power after the LDP's victory, sensed the political mood of the nation and publicly averred "... there is no room for negotiation".[19]

When a state attempts to exercise sovereignty over a territory, the first question that must be answered is whether the exercise of sovereignty is a break in precedent, or is in keeping with the status quo of the sovereignty in the dispute. If the exercise of sovereignty falls within the prevailing status quo, then this does not affect the sovereignty status and, thus, there is no requirement for any major protest. The primary goal of a state is to gain or maintain sovereignty over the disputed territory, which is achieved through the direct exercise of sovereignty over the territory in question and international recognition of this sovereignty. What is most significant is preventing the other state from doing the same. Utilising a constructivist understanding of sovereignty, the parties in question have sought to maintain/improve their position in the dispute's sovereignty status quo by effecting exercises of sovereignty over the disputed islands and associated waters, and preventing the other state from doing the same.[20] The sovereignty game framework is based on Alexander Wendt's conception of sovereignty as a social construction wherein he asserts that the modern concept of sovereignty is a socially constructed institution providing the "social basis for the individuality and security of states."

Sovereignty has two aspects: (1) recognition – which provides legitimacy; and (2) authority.

Authority is the ability to actually exercise sovereignty over the territory, or to prevent another state from doing so. Recognition and authority are two key aspects of how sovereignty comes into existence.[21] The final requirement for sovereignty is territoriality. As Thomson puts it, "With sovereignty, states mutually recognise exclusive authority over what is contained in that [bordered] space." The concepts of authority and recognition, which underpin the modern notion of sovereignty, are also the fundamental building blocks of the sovereignty game framework – in a territorial dispute, territoriality is quintessential. To sum up, the exercise of sovereignty forms the basis of the legal principle of effective control, in the absence of arbitration.[22] The escalation/de-escalation dichotomy leaves us bereft of an understanding of the dynamics of the dispute itself. While Japan enjoys effective control over the islands, could China attempt an overturn to this with the use of force?

In a world without sovereignty, the existence of the state does not have any basis in social recognition; there is no understanding that "a state has a right to its existence, territory and subjects", as averred famously by English political philosopher, Thomas Hobbes.[23] Hobbes asserted that there are two ways of identifying the sovereign in a society, as in a person or body of persons who have been given the right of governing through the social contract, or for that matter, have the three "marks" of sovereignty, namely, control of the military, ability to raise money, and control of religious doctrines. In another submission on the subject, Janice Thomson argues that "sovereignty is the recognition by internal and external actors that the state has the exclusive authority to intervene coercively in activities within its territory." While recognition provides legitimacy, it is this legitimacy which implies that other states will act to confirm the actions of the sovereign state over its recognised sovereign territory. However, Thomson herself admits that this is a problematic aspect of sovereignty. On the one hand, sovereignty is derived from the recognition of other states, but, on the other, states can exercise sovereignty without the recognition of other states.[24]

Role of Foreign Ministries

Further complicating the relationship between China and Japan and preventing effective management of crises, is the relative weakness of the Chinese Foreign Ministry, which is the official – and often the only – channel open to Tokyo. On the contrary, in Japan, the Foreign Ministry holds a higher position. Therefore there has been a mismatch in the relative power of the diplomats in both nations. In Japan, the Foreign Ministry division chief overseeing the China policy, directly briefs the Prime Minister. Conversely, in China, the State Councillor in charge of foreign policy is responsible for liaising with the senior leadership. Dai Bingguo was in that position until March 2013 and thereafter, Yang Jiechi, was elevated from the position of Foreign Minister "会议投票决定杨晶、常万全、杨

洁篪、郭声琨、王勇为国务委员", 新华社.[25] The State Councillor is one rank above the Foreign Minister and one rank below the Vice Premier – and is the highest-ranking official in charge of foreign affairs. A prominent reason for the Chinese Foreign Ministry's lack of authority is that domestic priorities, such as sustaining economic growth and political stability, still far outweigh foreign policy.[26] According to a Chinese analyst, "... the Diaoyu Islands may be the priority of Chinese foreign policy, but economic development is still the priority of overall Chinese policy".

A diminishing "China school" in the Japanese Foreign Ministry is also a significant factor driving the relationship to where it stands today. Japan's diplomacy with China has also suffered from the relative decline of a group within the Foreign Ministry known as the "China school", comprising specialists equipped with extensive China-specific experience and language skills. For many years, these diplomats headed the ministry's China and Mongolia Division as well as the Asian and Oceanic Affairs Bureau. These two departments, along with the Vice Foreign Minister, formed the core of China policy within the ministry. China school officials for a long time also served as Ambassadors to China and as heads of the Cabinet Councillors' Office on External Affairs. These individuals were professionally committed to Sino-Japanese relations and had "a vested institutional interest in avoiding conflict under their watch".[27] The China school began to lose its influence in the late 1990s due to a hardening of the public's attitude toward China and the chill in relations during the Koizumi era. In 2006, the Director of the China and Mongolia Division was not a Chinese language speaker – a first exception for that position – but was a specialist on the Japanese-US relationship. By the time Sino-Japanese relations entered their most challenging stretch in 2010, the traditional China school diplomats had lost influence, with their successors tending to take a tougher line on China.[28]

US-Japan Security Alliance and Regional Security in East Asia

The US National Security Strategy 2015 states that American alliances in Asia (with Japan, South Korea, Thailand, the Philippines and Australia) underwrite security throughout Asia and the Pacific, with the US-Japan alliance hinging on the principles of deterrence and balance of power, taking stock of the growing challenges from a rising China. Japan banks heavily on the United States' rebalancing its strategic attention and military forces towards the Asia-Pacific. It needs to be noted that the US and Japan together account for 28 per cent of the world's Gross Domestic Product (GDP) and 43 per cent of the world's wealth. The existing order in the Asia-Pacific holds critical pockets of uncertainty that could threaten both economic progress and political stability – with China's trajectory being the most uncertain variable in so far as shaping the security environment of the Asia-Pacific region out to 2030 is concerned. Regardless of China's economic trajectory, its investment in military capabilities is likely to continue, thus, the country's assertive behaviour and expansive claims to territory are unlikely to abate and could intensify.[29]

Since the end of World War II, any discussion on potential strategic options for Japan is considered a taboo topic. To put it simply, Japan arguably has had no viable options other than one, which can be considered strategically realistic and politically affordable, namely the Japan-US security alliance combined with the limited self-defence capability of the Japanese military forces. Today, 25 years have passed since the Cold War ended, and the Japan-US alliance remains the lynchpin of Tokyo's foreign and security strategy. Japan's psychological and material dependence on Washington has been deeply etched in the minds of a majority of the Japanese people. The history of the Japan-US alliance has had a profound impact not just on the modern history of Japan, but also on the broader international history of the Asia-Pacific region.[30]

Tracing its history, during the 1951 Treaty negotiations and in later years, Chief US delegate, John Foster Dulles and President Dwight Eisenhower, maintained that Japan would have "residual sovereignty" over the Ryukyu Islands, meaning "... the United States will not transfer its sovereign powers over the Ryukyu Islands to any nation other than Japan." Later, in 1962, President John Kennedy stated, "I recognize the Ryukyus to be a part of the Japanese homeland and look forward to the day when the security interests of the Free World will permit their restoration to full Japanese sovereignty."[31] Accordingly, the United States signed the Okinawa Reversion Treaty in June 1971, providing for the return of "all and any powers of administration, legislation and jurisdiction," over the Ryukyu and Daito Islands to Japan. Additionally, an Agreed Minute to the Okinawa Reversion Treaty confirmed that the boundaries of the Ryukyu and Daito Islands were "as designated under USCAR 27," which included the Senkaku Islands.[32] However, Article II of the Okinawa Reversion Treaty poses a notable exception to the United States' otherwise cautious policy towards the Senkaku/Diaoyu Islands. Article II states that those treaties, conventions, and other agreements concluded between Japan and the United States of America, including, but without limitation to the Treaty of Mutual Cooperation and Security between Japan and the United States of America... "become applicable to the Ryukyu Islands and the Daito Islands as of the date of entry into force of this Agreement". In other words, in the event of an armed attack on the Senkaku/Diaoyu Islands, the United States has an explicit security obligation to maintain the integrity of Japan's borders, including those islands for which it has only administrative rights. To corroborate Article II, the Okinawa Reversion Treaty further stipulates in Article V that each party would act "in accordance with its constitutional provisions and processes in response to an armed attack . . . in the territories under the *administration* of Japan."[33] Indeed, before the Senate was able to review and ratify the Okinawa Reversion Treaty in late 1971, the Nixon administration "removed the Senkakus from its inclusion in the concept of Japanese residual sovereignty." The State Department's Acting Assistant Legal Adviser for East Asian and Pacific Affairs, Robert Starr, stated in a letter dated October 20, 1971, "[t] he United Stated believes that a return of administrative rights over those islands to Japan, from which the rights were received, can in no way prejudice any underlying claims... The United States has made no claim to the Senkaku Islands and considers that any conflicting claims to the islands are a matter for resolution by the parties concerned."[34] Although the US does not take a stated position vis-à-vis the sovereignty status of the islands, given that Japan maintains administrative control over the Senkaku Shotō, it, nonetheless, subjects them to come under the US-Japan Security Treaty, which acts as a powerful deterrent against any/all use of force.[35]

Putting the above into context, it was under the terms of the Okinawa Reversion Treaty that the US handed back administrative rights to Okinawa prefecture, including the Senkaku Shotō in 1972. Successive US administrations, going back at least, to the Nixon administration, have stated that the United States takes no position on the territorial disputes. Interestingly, despite the on-going Cold War tensions at that time, President Richard Nixon's ambitious visit to the Communist People's Republic of China made him the first American President to pursue formal diplomatic relations with China in over 25 years. Many analysts and commentators believe that this sudden and significant shift in foreign policy caused the United States to backpedal and take a neutral position on the competing sovereignty claims over the Senkaku Islands. It has been US policy ever since 1972 that the 1960 US-Japan Security Treaty covers the islets, because Article 5 of the treaty stipulates that the United States is bound to protect "the territories under the administration of Japan" and Japan administers the Senkakus. Under the treaty, the United States guarantees Japan's security in return for the right to station US troops – which currently number around 50,000 in bases throughout the Japanese archipelago.[36] It is a less known fact that the privately owned Kuba Island and Japanese state-owned Taisho Island (both part of the Senkaku Islands), are under the exclusive control of the US military. The Japanese government made the decision to purchase three islands after Shintaro Ishihara, then Governor of Tokyo, announced his intention to purchase and develop them. At the time, a few key Japanese citizens criticised Ishihara for not also announcing his intention to purchase Kuba from its private owner. Ishihara explained that he was unable to purchase Kuba because the island, along with the state-owned Taisho Island, was still under the exclusive control of the US Navy, as outlined in the 1960 US-Japan Status of Forces Agreement (SOFA). The Japanese Ministry of Defence, since 1972, has been leasing Kuba to the US military as a bombing range along with Taisho.

Although both islands have not been used by the US military since 1978, and Article II (3) of SOFA states, "... the facilities and areas used by the United States armed forces shall be returned to Japan whenever they are no longer needed for purposes of this Agreement", they have not yet been returned to Japan.[37] The United States' management of the two islands implicitly places Washington as another actor in the Senkaku dispute.

However, what appeared to be causing strain in the US-Japan equation in the past few years was the expectation by Japan's political leadership that Washington would take a further step and openly support Japan's claim to the islands – a step that the Obama administration seemed unwilling to take since it perceivably did not want to further mess up its already knotty relationship with Beijing any more than it already was. When the Obama administration announced its pivot to Asia in late 2011 and early 2012, there was much consternation over the choice of words, with 'pivot' implying impermanence, and the preferred term soon became 'rebalance'. This only partially described the policy mix adopted by Washington. A more accurate phrase would have been a 'rebalance of burdens in Asia' as Christian Le Mière appositely argues, saying that pivot/rebalance is nothing but burden sharing (or burden-shifting) that aims to rebalance responsibility for security in Asia from the United States to its allies. Facing fiscal austerity, the US did find it challenging to bring into effect a wholesale shift in the weight of its forces to the Asia- Pacific, and thus, appeared to be encouraging its allies to assume a greater part of the burden of regional defence and security. At the heart of this rebalance came a strategic shift from land-based wars in West and South Asia to a focus on the maritime domain in East and Southeast Asia.[38] Along with an intense debate around the ability of the rebalance policy to deter, concurrent concerns about the policy's capacity to fulfill its other major goal, reassuring US allies in the region, too, cropped up. Burden sharing by devolution would not only mean Japan's primary role and responsibility in the defence of Japan, but also sharing the responsibilities for the maintenance of a stable international order. This would pave the way for a far more self-reliant defence posture and a gradual shift in Japan's defence capability toward the power-projection end of the force spectrum, and its more proactive involvement in international security affairs, both regionally and globally.[39]

Strategic Power Play

The previous and current leadership in China is seeking ways to leverage Beijing's growing military, diplomatic, and economic clout to advance its ambitions to establish regional preeminence and expand international influence. In this reference, the military-technological development of the People's Liberation Army and the tenets and probable development of Chinese security and military strategies over the next 20 years will leave an indelible impression on Asia's geo-strategic scene – perhaps a definitive and decisive one. The long-term, comprehensive modernisation of the armed forces of the People's Republic of China has entered a new phase since January 2016 as Beijing unveiled sweeping organisational reforms to overhaul the entire military structure. These reforms aim to strengthen the Chinese Communist Party's (CCP's) control over the military, enhance the PLA's ability to conduct joint operations, and improve its ability to fight short-duration, high-intensity regional conflicts at greater distances from the Chinese mainland.[40] The Chinese leaders fully comprehend that instability/conflict would substantially jeopardise China's peaceful external environment that has enabled its economic development in the past decades – a tenet that is central to the perpetuation of the CCP's domestic political legitimacy. That said, China, simultaneously has continued to assert sovereignty claims over features in the East and South China Seas. In the East China Sea, China continued to use maritime law enforcement ships and aircraft to patrol near the Senkaku Islands – viewed as a tacit move to enforce maritime claims, just below the threshold of provoking conflict.[41]

It is becoming nearly habitual for China to use a progression of small, incremental steps to increase its effective control over disputed areas in the land and maritime realms, and avoid escalation to limited or full-scale military conflict, while concomitantly maintaining a near-continuous presence in the disputed maritime, land area/areas to demonstrate its unceasing claim. In the long term, the Chinese leaders appear to be fixated on developing the capabilities they deem necessary to deter or defeat adversary power projection and counter the US' intervention during a crisis or conflict. In fact, the US Department of Defence has acknowledged in a 2016 declassified report (National Defense Authorization Act for Fiscal Year 2010, Public Law 111-84) that China's military modernisation is producing capabilities that hold the potential to reduce core US military technological advantages. With an expanding global footprint, China's military modernisation programme has become more focussed on investments and infrastructure to support a range of missions beyond China's periphery, including power projection and sea-lane security.

The emergence of China as a global actor presents a far-reaching challenge, especially for policy-makers in the region, given the on-going power shifts driven by China's growing comprehensive national power and influence. Japanese analysts argue that with this power shift that has been underway in the region, as China rises, the time has come for Japan to rethink its post-war strategic policy and consider its strategic options for the future: (1) the continuation of the status quo—the policy of keeping the US as the foundation of Japan's security strategy while maintaining a low profile defence posture; (2) a global civilian power option with proactive participation in international peace-building and security cooperation, especially in areas of non-traditional security issues; and (3) a normal state option—the policy of a self-reliant military posture with mature allied relations with the US and security partnerships with major powers in the world.[42]

The growing military and political assertiveness displayed by China in Asia, be it around the South China Sea, South Asia, or East Asia for that matter, has propelled the "China threat" debate and resulted in Tokyo's toughening China policy, and resultantly consolidated China's anti-Japanese stance as well. The most immediate and seeming challenge for Japan today, continues to be in its own neighbourhood. China's assertive claims to most of the East China Sea, coupled with the dramatic increase in the operational tempo of the PLA and other maritime services, including repeated circumnavigation of Japan, reveal Beijing's intention to assert greater strategic influence throughout the "First Island Chain" (referring to the first chain of major archipelagos out from the East Asian continental mainland coast, principally composed of the Kuril Islands, Japanese Archipelago, Ryukyu Islands, Taiwan, the northern Philippines, and Borneo) or what Beijing considers the "near sea." A Chinese strategic expert from the naval college opines, "If Japan totally controls the surrounding waters near the Diaoyu Islands, Chinese navy's critical access to the East China Sea would be blockaded."[43] Therefore, Chinese naval analysts see control of the islands as critical to accessing the Pacific Ocean beyond this "First Island Chain".[44] For Japan, the prospect of losing control over the Senkakus implies providing China a platform to monitor Japanese and US military activities in Okinawa, about 400 km in the east, and potentially curtailment of freedom of navigation to a great extent.

Lin Hongyu argues that at a strategic level, China must do everything to break through the encirclement created by the First Island Chain. By strengthening its sea power, and transforming itself from a "maritime nation" (海洋大国, *haiyang daguo*) to a "marine superpower" (海洋强国 *haiyang qiangguo*) China would protect its influence in the Pacific while creating a real deterrent against other Navies in the region. Lin contends that the 21st century belongs to the maritime powers, and China must develop maritime strength, which is proportionate to its economic power. Lin puts this in reference to what Sun Yat-Sen had stated of the 20th century being dominated by continental powers.[45] Meanwhile, Chu Shulong argues that, in the face of the "precarious maritime situation" (海洋困境, *haiyang kunjing*), China is not actually being "aggressive" (咄咄逼人, *duoduobiren*), but is, in fact, projecting "weakness" (软弱, *ruanruo*).[46] And, Jin Canrong opines that China is in a slight disadvantage to Japan in the East China Sea, but its regional position is gradually improving.[47] Believing that the US already benefits from two key advantages over Beijing, Liu Jianfei argues: (1) the US maintains an effective system of regional alliances; (2) the US is trying to legitimise its intervention in China's territorial disputes, hoping to fan the flames (煽风点火, *shanfeng dianhuo*) by relying on neighbouring countries. Liu Jianfei further states that the US involvement in the dispute allows it to legitimise its "pivot" to Asia. Proclaiming that the US is using territorial disputes as the "trump card to put pressure on China" (美国打压中国的一张牌, *Meiguo daya Zhongguo de yizhangpai*), former senior PLA officers regularly give vent to hardline rhetoric that borders dangerously, on war-mongering.[48]

Revision of US-Japan Defence Guidelines and Japan's Pacifist Constitution

China's regular deployment of government and other naval vessels in the East China Sea conveys a strong politico-military message, and has resulted in increased surveillance activities by the Japanese Self-Defence Force in recent years.[49] The Chinese marine surveillance ship *Haijian* No. 66 (c) cruising next to Japan Coast Guard patrol ships, and Chinese Coast Guard vessel Nos. 31239 and 2146 sailing in the East China Sea dangerously close to the Senkaku Islands, have become a regular feature of late. With Chinese activities such as these, Japan switched on a radar station in the East China Sea, enabling it permanent intelligence-gathering on the island of Yonaguni at the western extreme of a string of Japanese islands in the East China Sea [150 km (90 miles) south of the Senkaku Islands] "Until yesterday, there was no coastal observation unit west of the main Okinawa island... it was a vacuum we needed to fill," said Daigo Shiomitsu, Commander of the new base on Yonaguni [30 sq km (11 sq miles)] and home to 1,500 people, who mostly raise cattle and grow sugarcane.[50] For that matter, even Taiwanese Navy and Coast Guard Ships undertake round the clock patrols around the Senkaku Islands, with Taiwan having deployed the E2K aircraft [which does not violate the Air Defence Identification Zone (ADIZ)] primarily meant for surveillance purposes and providing support to targets that cannot be controlled by land-based radar sites. [As I discerned during the course of my interview with a Taiwanese Rear Admiral on board a KIDD-class Destroyer (Taiwanese Navy) at the Su'ao Naval Base, July 2015, Taiwan.]

The PLA Navy's increased presence in the South China Sea and East China Sea and shared theme of sovereignty further raise questions about Beijing's intentions over the Senkakus, making one thing rather certain—China's 'core interest' claims further reduces its diplomatic credibility in the region.[51] The concerns from a Japanese perspective remain that giving in on the Senkaku Islands would only lead the Chinese to aim next at undermining Japan's sovereignty over Okinawa – something that shall be absolutely unacceptable to the Japanese political leadership.[52] It is only pertinent to cite Beijing's forceful rhetoric, by none less than former Chinese Premier Wen Jiabao who stated that "... [China] would ... never yield an inch over the islands." Venting anger towards the United States in a White Paper released by the Information Office of the State Council in September 2012, titled *Diaoyu Dao, an Inherent Territory of China*:

> The United States and Japan conducted backroom deals concerning the "power of administration" over Diaoyu Dao ... the Taiwan authorities also expressed firm opposition to the backroom deal between the United States and Japan.[53]

While the US Navy and Japan's Maritime Self-Defense Forces (JMSDF) have historically led in bilateral interoperability, the new environment requires significantly greater jointness and interoperability across Services in both countries, individually, and bilaterally between the US and Japan.[54] What is important to note is that the distinction between the "defence of Japan" and "regional security" is thin. A sealed-off Strait of Hormuz or a military contingency in the South China Sea will have severe implications for the security and stability of Japan, requiring more robust, shared, and interoperable Intelligence, Surveillance, and Reconnaissance (ISR) capabilities and operations that extend well beyond Japanese territory. Former US Deputy Secretary of State, and naval officer, Richard L Armitage and Joseph S Nye argue that the US Forces in Japan (USFJ) should have specific roles assigned in the defence of Japan, with the goal of operational competency and eventual USFJ-JSDF (Japan Self-Defence Forces) joint task force capability. Washington, they assert, should allocate greater responsibility and sense of mission to the USFJ.[55]

Article 9 of the Japanese Constitution prohibits the use of force to resolve conflicts except in cases of self-defence. However, this reinterpretation of the law will now allow use of force to defend Japan's allies (the US) under attack, thus, making way for the Japanese forces to participate in defence operations around the globe. The road on this issue, however, is not expected to be smooth, given that the post-war pacifist identity is rooted profoundly in the minds and psyche of the Japanese people. Moreover, it casts a reflection on the political scene in Japan – in that, the decision to reinterpret the Constitution has yet to get a clearance from the opposition, so as to effectively become legislation. The ruling Liberal Democratic Party's coalition partner in the government, the Komeito – a political outfit drawing most of its membership from a steadfast Buddhist politico-religious grouping – has expressed reservations over this decision, more so, from the party's local units. Sensing this unwillingness, Prime Minister Shinzo Abe has made a canny move by choosing to use the term "reinterpreting", rather than "revising" the Constitution. By doing so, he has attempted to avoid the need for a public referendum on the subject, since the word "revision" evokes very strong sentiments in the public. In a Japanese Cabinet decision of July 01, 2014, measures for self-defence permitted under Article 9 of the Constitution were defined with the language of Article 9 of the Constitution appearing to prohibit "use of force" in international relations in all forms.

However, when considered in the light of "the right (of the people) to live in peace", as recognised in the Preamble of the Constitution, and the purpose of Article 13 of the Constitution which stipulates, "their (all the people's) right to life, liberty, and the pursuit of happiness" shall be the supreme consideration in governmental affairs, Article 9 of the Constitution cannot possibly be interpreted to prohibit Japan from taking measures of self-defence necessary to maintain the country's peace and security and ensure its survival. Such measures for self-defence are permitted only when they are inevitable for dealing with imminent unlawful situations where the people's right to life, liberty, and the pursuit of happiness is fundamentally overturned due to an armed attack by a foreign country, and for safeguarding these rights of the people. Hence, "use of force" to the minimum extent necessary to that end is permitted.[56] This logic must be maintained under Article 9 of the Constitution. To date, the government has considered that "use of force" under this basic logic is permitted only when an "armed attack" against Japan occurs. However, in the light of the situation in which the security environment surrounding Japan has fundamentally been transformed and is continuously evolving by shifts in the global power balance, the rapid progress of technological innovation, an armed attack occurring against a foreign country could actually threaten Japan's survival, depending on its purpose, scale and manner.

The revision of the US-Japan defence guidelines in April 2015, the first such amendment since 1997, became the flagship pronouncement during Japanese

Prime Minister Shinzo Abe's visit to the US in the same year. Review of the defence guidelines has sent out multiple signals simultaneously to East Asia, as Tokyo and Washington manifest the commitment of the US-Japan security alliance for Japan's domestic audience and across the region. It is only too well known that Abe staunchly favours Japan taking up a more proactive role and responsibility for the nation's security. Reforms in Japan's defence and foreign policy quarters under the Abe administration, including launching a national security strategy, creation of a national security council, revising national defence programme guidelines, and amending arms exports policies are portends of a far more hands-on approach that the Abe administration has embraced vis-à-vis Japan's overall security policy. For that matter, the resolution passed by the Japanese Cabinet in mid-2014, reinterpreting Japan's pacifist Constitution to allow the exercise of the right to collective self-defence was inferred to be a validating step in this direction.

With the announcement of revising the defence guidelines, the shift in the US-Japan security equation has become perceptible and can well be referenced in the context of the Obama administration's Asian rebalance. By aiding Japan's national security, the guidelines incline the alliance beyond Japan's immediate proximity to the broader Asia-Pacific region, and this purging of geographic restrictions shall redefine conceptual and operational extended deterrence and grey zones — the most perturbing of which is the East China Sea. It would not really be imprudent to argue that China has surreptitiously used the existing space of obscurity to its advantage in this sphere. Amidst a sea of strategic reverberations in the region, there needs to be greater clarity and less room for ambiguity in the US-Japan commitment to East Asian security, particularly over the Senkaku Islands. During Obama's visit to Japan in the spring of 2014, the internal political debate, including sections within the conservative ruling Liberal Democratic Party, began questioning the role of the US in the intensely contested Senkaku Islands dispute between Japan and China. While Obama had reassured about Washington's commitment to Japanese security in 2014, his tone was far more distinctive during Shinzo Abe's visit to the US in April 2015. Obama refrained from outlining Washington's policy of neutrality on the dispute – decoded to being a taciturn rebuke to China. On the other hand, Abe drew a full crowd when he addressed a joint session of the US Congress – the first by a Japanese leader. The speech was designed to ensure that Abe did not come across as a historical revisionist and remained committed to strengthening the US-Japan alliance.

By adopting a seemingly preemptive posture on security, Shinzo Abe is consolidating his conservative support base at home, while simultaneously dovetailing with the Obama administration's Asian rebalance precept. Abe's political campaign and strategy hinge on accentuating the strength of Japan's post-war liberalism, with a vision to rejuvenate Japan. Concurrently, Abe has chosen to steer Japan towards a regional order that puts up a challenge to China and its prophecy of Asian regionalism, in the backdrop of Beijing's growing military offensive. Revision of the defence guidelines has provided a fresh connotation to the US-Japan alliance, which has long been considered the keystone of Washington's security role in Asia, and the greater Asia-Pacific region.

The Japanese decision to counter China's aggression, both militarily and politically, cannot be considered and termed unfounded. Former President Hu Jintao told the 18th Congress of the Chinese Communist Party way back in November 2012, "We [China] should enhance our capacity for exploiting maritime resources, resolutely safeguard China's maritime rights and interests, and build China into a maritime power."[57] This is in clear reference to the overall picture of China strengthening its military forces broadly and rapidly by sustaining large increases in its defence budget. Simultaneously, its enhancing its asymmetric military capabilities to deter military forces of other countries from approaching, and advancing into regions that surround China, and to inhibit their military activities in the region by means of the Anti-Access/Area Denial (A2/AD) military strategy and capabilities.

Military-Technological Innovation and Reform in the PLA

During 2015-16, the PLA has continuously improved key capabilities that would be put into operation in theatre contingencies, including cruise missiles; short, medium, and intermediate-range ballistic missiles; high performance aircraft; integrated air defence networks; information operations capabilities; and amphibious and airborne assault units. The PLA is developing and testing new intermediate- and medium-range conventional ballistic missiles as well as long-range, land-attack, and anti-ship cruise missiles, which, once operational, would extend the military's reach and push adversary forces further from potential regional conflicts. Besides, China is also focussing on counter-space, offensive cyber operations, and Electronic Warfare (EW) capabilities meant to deny adversaries the advantages of modern, information technology-driven warfare.[58]

PLA Rocket Force (PLARF)

The revamped Rocket Force (the PLA's erstwhile Second Artillery Corps) operates China's land-based nuclear and conventional missiles. Since 2015, China has been stressing on a more dispersed and survivable capability by means of nuclear-capable delivery systems in its missile forces and Navy. The Rocket Force today is developing and testing several new classes and variants of offensive missiles, including test-launching a hypersonic glide vehicle in 2014; Manoeuvrable Reentry

Vehicles (MaRVs), Multiple Interdependly Targetable Reentry Vehicles(MiRVs), decoys, chaff, jamming, and thermal shielding. It is also forming additional missile units, upgrading older missile systems, and developing methods to counter ballistic missile defences. The force possesses approximately 1,200 Short-Range Ballistic Missiles (SRBMs) in its inventory.[59] China is increasing the lethality of its conventional missile force by fielding the CSS-11 (DF-16) ballistic missile with a range of 800-1,000 km. The CSS-11, coupled with the already deployed conventional land-attack and anti-ship variants of the CSS-5 (DF-21C/D) Medium-Range Ballistic Missile (MRBM), will improve China's ability to strike not only Taiwan, but other regional targets as well. These ballistic missile systems are complemented by the CJ-10 Ground-Launched Cruise Missile (GLCM). The CJ-10 has a range in excess of 1,500 km and offers flight profiles different from ballistic missiles that can enhance targeting options. China is fielding a growing number of conventionally armed MRBMs, including the CSS-5 Mod 5 (DF-21D) Anti-Ship Ballistic Missile (ASBM). The CSS-5 Mod 5, with a range of 1,500 km and a manoeuvrable warhead, gives the PLA the capability to attack ships, including aircraft carriers, in the western Pacific Ocean.[60]

More recently, China unveiled the DF-26 Intermediate-Range Ballistic Missile (IRBM) during the September 2015 parade in Beijing. When fielded, the DF-26 will be capable of conducting precision strikes against ground targets, and will contribute to strategic deterrence in the Asia-Pacific region. The official parade announcer also referenced a nuclear version of the DF-26, which, if sharing similar guidance capabilities, would give China its first nuclear precision strike capability against theatre targets. Enhancing its silo-based Inter-Continental Ballistic Missiles (ICBMs) and adding more survivable, mobile delivery systems, China's ICBM arsenal to date consists of approximately 75-100 ICBMs, including the silo-based CSS-4 Mod 2 (DF-5) and MiRV-equipped Mod 3 (DF-5B); the solid-fuelled, road-mobile CSS-10 Mod 1 and 2 (DF-31 and DF-31A); and the shorter range CSS-3 (DF-4). The CSS-10 Mod 2, with a range in excess of 11,200 km, can reach most locations within the continental United States. China also is developing a new road-mobile ICBM, the CSS-X-20 (DF-41) capable of carrying MiRVs.[61]

PLA Navy (PLAN)

Over the past 15 years, the ambitious naval modernisation programme of the PRC has resulted in the PLA Navy now possessing the largest number of vessels in Asia, with more than 300 surface ships, submarines, amphibious ships, and patrol craft. China is rapidly inducting multi-mission ships equipped with advanced anti-ship, anti-air, and anti-submarine weapons and sensors. The PLAN places high priority on the modernisation of its submarine force. In the two categories of nuclear-powered submarines: i.e., ballistic missile submarines and attack submarines, the PLAN currently possesses five nuclear-powered attack submarines (SSNs) and four Jin-class nuclear-powered ballistic missile submarines (SSBNs) that are currently operational. In a Congressional testimony, cited in the 2016 Pentagon report, former US Pacific Command Commander, Adm Samuel Locklear said that China might build up to eight Type 094s SSBNs. In addition, the PLAN has 53 diesel-powered attack submarines (SSs/SSPs). It is estimated that by 2020, this force will likely grow to between 69 and 78 submarines.[62] In addition to the 12 KILO-class SS units acquired from Russia in the 1990s and 2000s, China has built 13 SONG-class SSs (Type 039) and 13 YUAN-class SSPs (Type 039A) with a total of 20 YUANs planned for production. China continues to improve its SSN force, and four additional SHANG-class SSNs (Type 093) will eventually join the two already in service. The SHANG SSN will replace the ageing HAN-class SSN (Type 091). These improved SHANG SSNs feature a Vertical Launch System (VLS) and may be able to fire the YJ-18 advanced Anti-Ship Cruise Missile (ASCM).[63]

Over the next decade, China is expected to begin constructing a new Type 095 nuclear-powered, guided-missile attack submarine (SSGN), which not only would improve the PLAN's anti-surface warfare capability but may also provide it with a more clandestine land-attack option. Finally, China continues to produce the JIN-class SSBN (Type 094) with the associated CSS-N-14 (JL-2) Submarine-Launched Ballistic

Missiles (SLBMs) that has an estimated range of 7,200 km. This platform represents China's first credible, sea-based nuclear deterrent. China's advancing nuclear deterrent was testified when it sent a Type 094 Jin-class SSBN out on its first deterrent patrol and by conducting a fifth reported test of its mobile, solid-fuel, MiRV-capable DF-41 ICBM. Although the first second-generation Type 094 (three of them are now based at the new large PLAN base at Yalong Bay on Hainan Island) was launched in 2004, *IHS Jane's Fighting Ships* reported that its premier deterrent patrol had not occurred until December 2015. "Given China's known capabilities and their efforts to develop a sea-based deterrent, in the absence of indicators to the contrary, it is prudent to assume that patrols are occurring," said the US Strategic Command spokesperson in a statement to *The Washington Times* published on December 10, 2015. The Type 094 SSBN is armed with 12 JL-2 Submarine-Launched Ballistic Missiles (SLBMs) armed with single nuclear warheads, ranging 7,000-8,000 km.[64] In succession to the Type 094 class SSBN will be the Type 096 in the coming decade. The Type 096 will reportedly be armed with a successor to the JL-2, the JL-3 SLBM – providing China with its first reliable long-range sea-based nuclear capability. JIN SSBNs based at Hainan Island in the South China Sea would then be able to conduct nuclear deterrence patrols.[65]

Augmenting the PLAN's littoral warfare capabilities, especially in the South China Sea and

East China Sea, is a new class of small combatants. Twenty-five JIANGDAO-class corvettes (FFL) (Type 056) are in service and the latest ships have been upgraded to Anti-Submarine Warfare (ASW) variants with towed array sonar. China may build more than 60 of this class, ultimately replacing older PLAN destroyers and frigates. China also has 60 HOUBEI-class wave-piercing catamaran guided-missile patrol boats (PTG) (Type 022) built for operations in China's "near seas."[66] China's investment in its amphibious ship force is apparent with the building of three large YUZHAO-class (Type 071) amphibious transport docks (LPD) with a fourth soon to enter service, providing considerably greater and more flexible capability for "far seas" operations than the older landing ships. The YUZHAO can carry up to four of the new YUYI-class air-cushion medium landing craft (LCMA) and four or more helicopters, as well as armoured vehicles and marines for long-distance deployments. Additional YUZHAO construction is expected in the near-term, as is a follow-on amphibious assault ship that is not only larger, but incorporates a full flight deck for helicopters. Two YUTING II-class tank landing ships (LST) are currently being built to replace older LST units that are reaching the end of their service lives, and to support logistics operations, particularly in the South China Sea.[67]

China's A2/AD Strategy: Disequilibrium for Regional Deterrence

The US' military power is dependent upon projecting power and access through bases to the theatre of operations, being reliant on a long logistical chain. On the contrary, China is operating in its own backyard and has consistently sought to exploit this fact and prevent Japan and the United States from accessing, as well as manoeuvring within, a theatre of operation – frequently referred to as the Anti-Access and Area-Denial (A2/AD) military strategy. The A2/AD is traditionally employed by a weaker party in an attempt to offset the military superiority of an adversary – relying on exploiting the cost-benefit ratio. By attempting to slow, limit, deny or deter a superior technologically advanced opponent from conducting threatening military operations, China's A2/AD systems and architectures have primarily been designed to "make power projection increasingly risky... and prohibitively costly"[68] given that A2/AD capabilities could compel US forces to operate with higher levels of risk and at greater distances from the theatre. Seeking to steadily expand the PLA's operational flexibility with rising numbers of mobile ICBMs in China's rocket inventory coupled with SSBN deterrence patrols, the PLA capabilities to project power shall notch up no doubt, however, it shall also call for implementing more sophisticated Command and Control (C2) systems and processes that safeguard the integrity of nuclear release authority for a larger, more dispersed force. The PLA's Missile and

Air Forces remain a critical component in extending China's defensive perimeter, as it frees up and enables other military assets to focus on conducting offensive missions, such as blockades, sovereignty enforcement, and/or A2/AD, farther from China's shores.[69]

The foundational basis of the A2/AD strategy is denying access, and ability, for the adversary to manoeuvre, near and within, a military theatre of operation.[70] Anti-Access (A2) refers to action, usually long-range, that is intended to slow/prevent deployment of forces into a theatre or cause forces to operate from distances farther from the locus of conflict than they would otherwise prefer – thus, affecting *movement towards* a theatre. Area-Denial (AD) refers to action, usually short-range, intended to impede operations within areas where the adversary cannot/will not prevent access – thus, affecting *manoeuvre within* a theatre. The A2/AD strategy goes beyond a singularly defined/identified theatre of operation, and could cause a delay in the deployment of US and Japanese forces in that theatre – thereby then forcing them to operate from longer distances, which could prove unfavourable from a military operational point of view. The A2/AD is a destabilising strategy in so far as maintaining regional deterrence in Asia and the Pacific is concerned. China seeks to enhance its own deterrent at the cost of lowering the deterrent value of the US and Japan in East Asia – for which, ceding one domain to China invites the eventual loss of the other interdependent domains. The US has often argued that it is not a guest in the Asia-Pacific theatre, but a Pacific nation with states, territories, and allies, whose continued prosperity, security, and protection is a commitment that America is bound to.

China's A2/AD seemingly poses a grave challenge to the US and Japanese forces in East Asia, comprising a fusion of new generation of anti-submarine warfare, cruise, ballistic, air-to-air, and surface-to-air missiles with improved ranges, accuracy, and lethality [hitting forward bases at ranges exceeding 1,000 nautical miles (1,852 km)] anti-satellite weapons, coupled with modern ultra-quiet diesel submarines and fighter aircraft, and over 80,000 sea mines being equipped with mobility and autonomy.[71] Of late, Beijing has consistently built up to strengthen its A2/AD platforms significantly, including preliminary efforts to develop sonar nets in the Yellow, East and South China Seas, thus, targeting the US Navy's attack submarines.[72] Besides, China has confirmed purchase of the Russian S-400 air defence platform, and has continued interest in the Su-35 fighter, Russian airplane engines, and ultra-quiet submarines and technology. For that matter, even low-technology capabilities, such as rudimentary sea mines, fast-attack small craft, or shorter-range artillery and missile systems render transit, into and through, the commons vulnerable to interdiction by coercive, aggressive actors, slowing or stopping free movement.[73]

The growing capabilities of the Chinese PLA would strengthen its A2/AD strategy and pose an increasing threat to US and Japanese bases and to their forces operating inside what China describes as its "First and Second Island Chains". East Asian waters are slowly but surely becoming a potential no-go zone for US ships, particularly for aircraft carriers, thus, risking the forward deployment of US military forces becoming "wasting assets."[74]

With greater impetus and investments in Beijing's missile technology, the A2/AD capabilities are an attempt to transform the area from China's coastline out to the First Island Chain into a "no-go" zone for US and allied forces – and eventually extend its anti-access abilities all the way to the Second Island Chain. The area within China's First Island Chain is a fiercely contested zone for operations – a line through the Kuril Islands, Japan, the Ryukyu Islands, Taiwan, the Philippines, and Indonesia (Borneo to Natuna Besar). The Second Island Chain runs from a north-south line from the Kurils through Japan, the Bonins, the Marianas, the Carolines, and Indonesia. Together, they encompass a maritime area out to approximately 1,800 nautical miles from China's coast, crucially including most of the East China Sea and East Asian SLOCs. It needs to be noted that the Island Chain concept has never been defined or drawn publicly by any official Chinese source.[75]

Fig 5.1: China's purported "First and Second Island Chain"

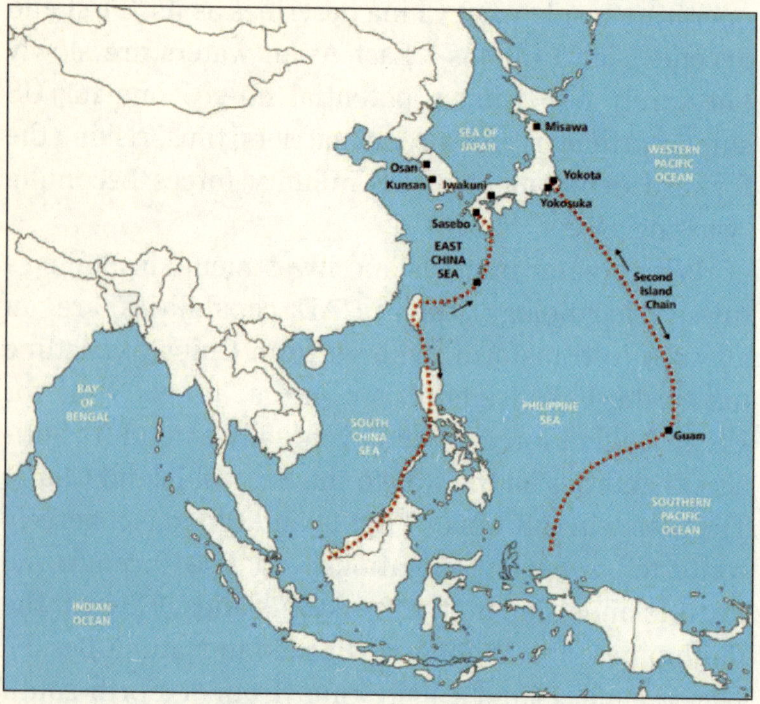

Source: As cited in, "China's ADIZ is a Strategic Move to Control First Island Chain," Consortium of Defense Analysts, December 25, 2013, available at https://cofda.files.wordpress.com/2013/12/1st-and-2nd-island-chains.jpg

Chinese Assertiveness in the East China Sea Maritime Domain

With the aim to build up capabilities to conduct operations in more distant waters and air space, China's expanding maritime activities based on sea power and air power, both qualitatively and quantitatively, are causing alarm regionally. The sea areas and air space surrounding Japan have observed Chinese naval vessels and Navy and Air Force aircraft (including ones belonging to the maritime law enforcement agencies) conducting training exercises such as carrier-based helicopter flights, fleet formation and manoeuvre exercises, as well as robust surveillance activity. In January 2013, it was reported that China planned to build 36 maritime law enforcement ships by 2018. Concerning the PLA, there is a view that by turning exception into normality through uniform peace-time and war-time force deployment and exceeding traditional activity spaces, China intends to desensitise the alertness of others and make the international community accept the changed scenario.[76] Surveillance and other activities in the seas were conducted by "Maritime Police" (*Haijing*) of the Ministry of Public Security, "China Maritime Surveillance" (*Haijian*) of the State Oceanic Administration of the Ministry of Land and Resources, "China Fisheries Law Enforcement Command" (*Yuzheng*) of the Bureau of Fisheries of the Ministry of Agriculture, "Maritime Safety Administration (*Haixun*)" of the Ministry of Transport, and the maritime anti-smuggling force of the General Administration of Customs, all of which come directly under the State Council. However, in March 2013, China decided to reorganise the four agencies, excluding the "Maritime Safety Administration" into the new State Oceanic Administration – with the mandate to carry out surveillance and other activities under the name of "China Coast Guard (*Zhongguo Haijing*)" and the guidance of the Ministry of Public Security. In July of the same year, the China Coast

Guard was formally launched, and it is believed that the State Committee of Border and Coastal Defence, under the guidance of the State Council and the Central Military Commission, is tasked to coordinate maritime activities by these maritime law-enforcement agencies and the Navy.

For that matter, Chinese naval fleets have been passing the sea area between the main island of Okinawa and Miyako Island regularly, every year, since 2008. With regard to the activities of Chinese government vessels (Chinese ships being termed as *kaikei* with *kai* meaning 'sea' and *kei* meaning 'policing'), in December 2008, "China Maritime Surveillance" vessels belonging to the State Oceanic Administration (SOA) of the Ministry of Land and Resources of China hovered near, and then drifted inside, Japan's territorial waters near the Senkaku Islands – operations which are not permitted under international law. Subsequently, in August 2011, as well as in March and July 2012, "China Maritime Surveillance" vessels and "China Fisheries Law Enforcement Command" vessels belonging to the (then) Bureau of Fisheries of the Ministry of Agriculture of China intruded into Japan's aforementioned territorial waters. In February 2012, a survey vessel of the Japan Coast Guard conducting a marine survey in Japan's EEZ was ordered to stop the activity by two "China Maritime Surveillance" ships belonging to the SOA (with similar incidents having occurred earlier in May and September 2010). In April 2012, a naval fleet passed the Osumi Strait eastward for the first time, and in October of the same year, navigated the sea area between Yonaguni Island and Nakanokami Island near Iriomote Island northward, again in a first such instance. In October 2012, vessels of the East Sea Fleet of the Chinese Navy and "China Maritime Surveillance" and "China Fisheries Law Enforcement Command" vessels conducted a joint exercise with a focus on maintaining and defending China's territorial sovereignty and maritime interests. As these examples demonstrate, "China Maritime Surveillance" and "China Fisheries Law Enforcement Command" vessels have gradually intensified their activities in Japan's territorial waters, especially after September 2012, when the Japanese government acquired property rights to, and ownership of, three of the Senkaku Islands (Uotsuri Island, Kitakojima Island, and Minamikojima Island).

In January 2013, a Chinese naval vessel directed fire-control radar at a JMSDF destroyer and is suspected to have directed fire-control radar at a helicopter based on the JMSDF destroyer.[77] Although the JJMSDF is the smallest of Japan's military branches, technologically, it is far more advanced than the PLAN. Yet, in the long-run, the JMSDF and the Japanese Coast Guard (JCG) – Tokyo's principle enforcer of maritime law – are at a relative disadvantage – in comparison to the bourgeoning naval rearmament programme of China, which is gradually shifting the regional maritime balance in Beijing's favour. "From a military perspective, Tokyo is becoming the weaker party in the Sino-Japanese rivalry," argues Naval War College Professor Toshi Yoshihara, and further states, "While the Ryukyus fall well inside the PLA's anti-access zone, the archipelago's strategic location offers Japan a chance to turn the tables on China. By deploying A2/AD units along the islands, Japanese defenders could slam shut an important outlet for Chinese surface, submarine and air forces into the Pacific high seas."[78] In April and September 2013, eight Chinese government vessels intruded into the territorial waters simultaneously.[79] Chinese naval fleets passed the Soya Strait eastward for the first time in July 2013. As such, the Chinese naval fleets' advancement and homing routes between the East China Sea and the Pacific Ocean continue to become diverse by incorporating the areas north of Japan, and it is understood that China seeks to improve its deployment capabilities to the open ocean. Furthermore, in October 2013, China reportedly conducted "Maneuver 5," the first joint exercise by its three naval fleets in the western Pacific Ocean. Chinese naval vessels appear to routinely conduct operations in the East China Sea. After referring to its own position regarding the Senkaku Islands, China alleges that patrols by Chinese naval vessels in the sea areas under its jurisdiction are completely justifiable and lawful. Furthermore, the Navy is believed to be supporting maritime law enforcement agencies in terms of both operation and equipment, including handing over retired Navy vessels to the China Coast Guard that was formally launched in July 2013.

Fully comprehending the significance of sea lines of communication, which serve as commercial trade routes in peace-time and become strategic lines of communication during war, China remains focussed on the Asia-Pacific with its two significant sea lines of communication: one, passing through the South China Sea to the Indian Ocean and West Asia; and the second, passing through the East China Sea and the Sea of Japan to the Pacific Ocean and the Pacific coast of the US and Canada. There are several straits of strategic importance in the region, such as the Straits of Malacca, Sunda, Lombok and Makassar in Southeast Asia, and the Straits of Tsushima, Tsugaru, Osumi, and Soya (La Perouse) in Northeast Asia. Major shipping routes in the Asia Pacific are through these key straits, which could be potential chokepoints.[80] At the first plenary meeting of the PLA during the 4th session of the 12th National People's Congress (NPC) on March 7, 2016, the Chinese military's increasing overseas military operations, including port calls to foreign countries, were highlighted, as they would "consolidate the Chinese military's position as a mighty force". Dai Shaoan proposed that it is necessary to accelerate national legislation and law on Chinese military's overseas military operations. Dai argued the same for long-distance transportation of troops, weapons and equipment for Chinese military's overseas military operations.[81]

The Japanese Coast Guard closely surrounds the island with around 7/8 vessels (round the clock).

To provide support to the Japanese Coast Guard, the Japanese destroyers are deployed in rotation at a distance of approximately 100 nautical miles – interpreted as a measure to prevent crisis escalation and prevent Chinese naval ships coming close to the Senkakus. For that matter, to place a check on Taiwanese fighter jets coming to Yonaguni Islands, the Japanese government changed the ADIZ to Yonaguni Islands (with the Senkakus being very close to the ADIZ line). Apparently, Taiwanese E2K planes come right till the line of Japan's ADIZ, but do not cross it, as the Japanese fighters approach to verify whether the approaching aircraft is friendly or not. Japan maintains that China is violating the Japanese ADIZ and attempting to challenge the existing status quo.[82]

China's Declaration of East China Sea Air Defence Identification Zone: Activities in Japan's Surrounding Air Space

Japan is composed of a little over 6,800 islands, and is surrounded by a wide region of sea, which includes the sixth largest Exclusive Economic Zone (EEZ) in the world. The SDF is engaged in round-the-clock intelligence gathering, and warning and surveillance in Japan's territorial waters and air space in peace time, as well as the surrounding sea and air space, so that it can respond in a timely and appropriate manner to a variety of situations. Beijing has jettisoned its erstwhile "low profile" international posture and has instead become more aggressive in pushing for its own narrowly defined national interests. With the official defence White Paper adding the phrase "air vigilance and patrols at sea" for the first time ever, China has intensified the activities of its aircraft, including fighters and the Chinese Ministry of National Defence has made public the fact that Chinese military aircraft and fighters regularly conduct warning and surveillance activities believed to be Combat Air Patrols (CAPs) in the East China Sea.

Since September 2007, multiple H-6 bombers advanced near the Japan-China median line followed by a Y-8 early warning aircraft advancing near the same line in March 2010. A year later, in March 2011, a Y-8 patrol aircraft and Y-8 intelligence gathering aircraft crossed the Japan-China median line and approached approximately within 50 km of the Japanese air space near the Senkaku Islands. In March and April 2011 and April 2012, Chinese helicopters that appeared to belong to the SOA flew close to JMSDF destroyers, which were engaged in monitoring and surveillance in the East China Sea. More specifically, on March 7, 2011, a Chinese Z-9 helicopter believed to belong to the SOA flew as close as approximately 70 m and as low as approximately 40 m above the water around the Japanese destroyer *Samidare*, which was patrolling waters in the central area of the East China Sea. On March 26, a Z-9 helicopter flew again as close as approximately 90 m and as low as approximately 60 m above the water around the destroyer *Isoyuki*. Furthermore, on April

1, a Y-12 aircraft that was believed to belong to the SOA flew as close as approximately 90 m and as low as approximately 60 m above the water around *Isoyuki*. On April 12, 2012, a Y-12 aircraft, believed to belong to the SOA flew approximately 50 m and as low as approximately 50 m above the water around the destroyer *Asayuki*. Regarding Japan's air space over and around the Senkaku Islands, in December 2012, a fixed-wing aircraft belonging to the SOA violated the territorial air space first as a Chinese aircraft. Since then, fixed-wing aircraft belonging to the SOA have been frequently observed flying near the air space.[83] On November 16 and 17, 2013, a Tu-154 intelligence gathering aircraft flew over the East China Sea on two consecutive days.[84] All this activity demonstrates that China has been further intensifying the activities of its aircraft, including fighters in the East China Sea air space.

In what appeared to being a frantic yet brawny attempt to create a fresh status quo in all its territorial disputes, the Chinese government announced establishing an East China Sea ADIZ on November 23, 2013, at 1000 hours, local time in China. The Ministry of National Defence of the People's Republic of China issued a statement claiming that the East China Sea ADIZ had been established in accordance with the Law of the People's Republic of China on National Defence (March 14, 1997), the Law of the People's Republic of China on Civil Aviation (October 30, 1995) and the Basic Rules on Flight of the People's Republic of

China (July 27, 2001). China's declaration of this ADIZ has surely upped the ante in this bitterly contested and explosive zone covering the Senkaku Islands, which remains under Japan's administrative control, in addition to the greater part of the East China Sea, including sections of Taiwan and South Korea – thereby infuriating the region. This provocative announcement by the Chinese government on areas including the Senkaku Islands, made it appear as if they were a part of China's "territory," that it obligated aircraft flying in the said zone to abide by the rules set forth by the Chinese Ministry of National Defence, and that the Chinese armed forces would take "defensive emergency measures" in the case of aircraft not following the instructed procedures.

Japan, expectedly, was deeply concerned about such measures, which remain profoundly dangerous acts that attempt to unilaterally change the existing status quo in the East China Sea, escalating the situation, causing unintended consequences in the East China Sea. The measures unduly infringe the freedom of overflight over the high seas, which is the general principle of international law. Japan is demanding that China revoke any measures that could infringe upon the freedom of overflight over the high seas. On the very day that China announced the establishment of the East China Sea ADIZ, a Tu-154 intelligence gathering aircraft and a Y-8 intelligence gathering aircraft flew over the East China Sea. On the same day, the Chinese Air Force announced that it conducted its first patrol flight since the establishment of the ADIZ. Subsequently, the Chinese armed forces announced on November 28 that a KJ-2000 Airborne Early Warning and Control System (AWACS) and Su-30 and J-11 fighters conducted patrol flights in the ADIZ, and announced on the following day that its Su-30 and J-11 fighters had scrambled. On December 26, 2013, the Chinese armed forces announced that in the one month that had passed since the establishment of the ADIZ, a total of 87 reconnaissance aircraft, early warning aircraft and fighters were mobilised to the relevant air space.[85] China's announcement of the ADIZ is part of a strategy that would aid in establishing its superiority and leverage in existential territorial and boundary disputes. It would also expand Beijing's long-term access to the Western Pacific.

Fig 5.2: The People's Republic of China, Air Defence Identification Zone (ADIZ) over the East China Sea

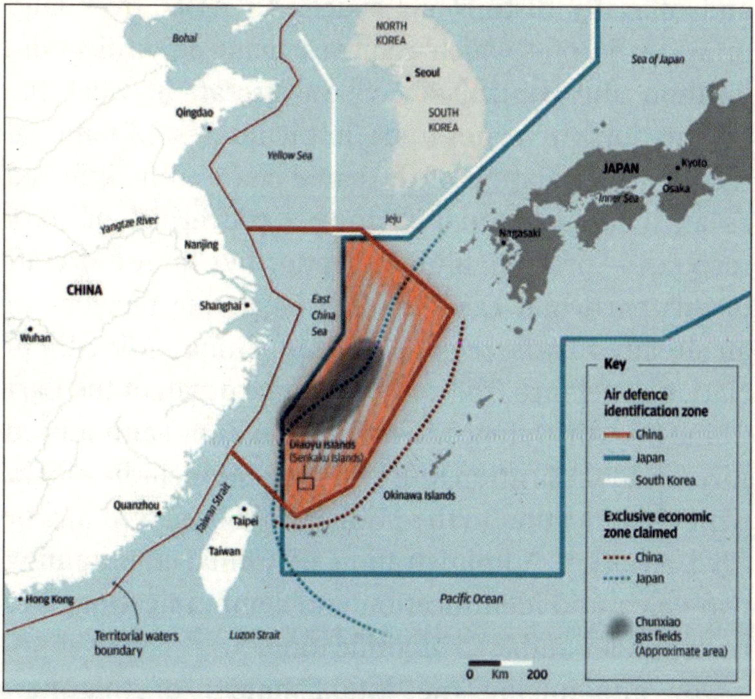

Source: People's Republic of China, Ministry of National Defence release, cited in, *South China Morning Post*, November 27, 2013.

To begin with, it needs to be understood as to what does an air defence identification zone denote? Being an early warning air defence concept used by nations since the 1960s in what is referred to as "uncontested air space" to enhance airborne security, an air defence identification zone differs from what is generally referred to as 'air space'. According to international law, while air space encompasses the sky above a territory plus 12 nautical miles (22 km) of coastal waterways, an ADIZ is a self-regulating means, by which a country can identify and monitor aircraft approaching its territory and officially distinct air space. An ADIZ over land or water is one which requires ready identification, location and control of civilian aircraft in what the host nation often cites to be 'in the interest of national security'. A violation of the same can well be inferred as an incursion, thus, eliciting a proverbial military response – presumably interception by Chinese aircraft in this particular case, thereby escalating tensions in an already volatile regional setting. China's Ministry of National Defence (the administrative organ of the East China Sea Air Defence Identification Zone) announced Aircraft Identification Rules for the zone including flight plan identification to the Ministry of Foreign Affairs or Civil Aviation Administration of China, maintaining two-way radio identification and communication, and transponder and logo identification.[86]

By announcing the establishment of this new ADIZ, China appears to be putting to test its military modernisation efforts of the past three decades. However, what remains to be seen is how China intends to undertake patrols and invoke its ADIZ, and more importantly, as far as enforcement is concerned, would China be able to monitor all of the desired air space? This mission can only be fulfilled while blending ground-based, naval and airborne systems. There certainly would be concerns pertaining to the Chinese capabilities, which are limited primarily because the mainland ground-based systems used to cover the ADIZ are much farther away, thus, making Beijing heavily dependent on airborne early warning systems. The most important in this entire chain of events in the East China Sea remains the Chinese attempt at force projection. While civilian aircraft flying through the ADIZ might just not be the foremost issue, the real alarm surrounds the trajectory of military flights.[87]

A2/AD, Air Sea Battle (ASB) and ADIZ can best be described as a cascading military approach / reaction cycle in the East China Sea, with each being a reactionary response to the former. ADIZ, seemingly, is part of China's A2/AD strategy in the East China Sea, which attempts to push US forces back and regulate its near seas and air space. This amplifies larger concerns over Chinese intentions throughout the Asia-Pacific and wider Indo-Pacific regions – including that over the Indian state of Arunachal Pradesh, which China claims as "Southern Tibet".

The Chinese media has underscored that "it requires both China and Japan to act in a wise and rational way, so as to prevent an escalation of conflict after China established the ADIZ" — thereby reinforcing that there is no possibility of a withdrawal by Beijing on the ADIZ. Instead of seeking to strike a balance and assuage the concern in the region regarding its robust military offensive, the China's leadership's actions are in sharp contrast as it continues to wrangle with an acerbic attitude and stance on sensitive strategic issues. On another front, the South Korean Defence Ministry regretted that China's ADIZ partly overlaps in 20 km width and 115 km length with the Korean ADIZ to the west of Jeju Island — to cover the Socotra Rock (Ieodo or Parangdo), presently under South Korean control but contested by China. The South Korean-controlled Ieodo, 149 km southwest of Korea's southernmost island of Marado, is a submerged rock that lies within the overlapping economic zones of Beijing and Seoul. Deductions stemming out of statements from South Korea suggest that establishment of the air defence identification zone by China shall not affect Seoul's jurisdiction over Ieodo.[88]

China, by virtue of its offensive posturing, has triggered a chain of responses from regional players. Japan has stepped up air surveillance in the East China Sea by stationing E-2C airborne early-warning aircraft at the Naha base in the Okinawa region and intensifying the use of unmanned Global Hawk aircraft. In May and June 2014, two Su-27 fighters of China flew abnormally close to the aircraft of the JMSDF and JASDF that were conducting routine monitoring and surveillance activities in the East China Sea. The Chinese Ministry of National Defence announced that JSDF aircraft conducted dangerous acts against Chinese aircraft. However, the operations of the JSDF aircraft were legitimate activities in compliance with international law. There is no veracity to the Chinese assertion that the JSDF aircraft carried out dangerous acts. With respect to Air Forces' advancement into the Pacific Ocean, it was confirmed for the first time by the JASDF's scrambling fighters that a Y-8 early warning aircraft and an H-6 bomber flew through the air space between the main island of Okinawa and Miyako Island and advanced to the Pacific Ocean in July and September 2013. Similar flights were conducted by two Y-8 early-warning aircraft, and two H-6 bombers (total: four aircraft) on three consecutive days in October 2013, and, thereafter by one Y-8 intelligence-gathering aircraft and two H-6 bombers (total: three aircraft) in March 2014.

Tensions in the region are certainly rife with responses to the declaration of the ADIZ, including two US B-52 bombers sent in from the military base in Guam flying through the Chinese ADIZ over the Senkaku Islands without identifying themselves/ notifying the Chinese authorities — something that China would have expected under the new regulations. Washington sent a clear signal to Beijing regarding its treaty commitments to Tokyo. Besides, the US Navy's first two advanced P-8A Poseidon patrol aircraft arrived in December 2013 in Japan. Equipped with the latest radar equipment and armed with torpedoes and anti-ship missiles, the long range maritime multi-mission aircraft with deployments to the US 7th Fleet Area of Responsibility (AOR)—with the third rotation of the type on-going at Kadena Air Base in Okinawa—the P-8A has greater capacity to stay out on a mission for a much longer time than the Lockheed Martin P-3 Orion patrol aircraft. Since completing the transition to the Poseidon from the P-3C in early 2014, a typical deployment to Kadena lasts between six to seven months, and currently consists of a single squadron of Lockheed Martin P-3C Orions and one of P-8As to demonstrate the ability of the two platforms to operate effectively.[89] It will be known, as more time goes by, whether the Chinese declaration of this air defence identification zone holds much ground, or comprises mere political and military symbolism to placate rising domestic nationalist responses. Given that this decision came soon after the conclusion of the Third Plenum of the 18th Central Committee of the Chinese Communist Party in Beijing, which set forth a grand agenda for reform, including national security, it might just be that Xi Jinping's administration is pitching for domestic support on its foreign policy agenda. There can, however, be no denying that the announcement of an air defence identification zone is part of China's larger A2/AD strategy that would aid in establishing its superiority and leverage in existential territorial and boundary disputes while simultaneously expanding Beijing's long-term access to the Western Pacific.[90]

Utilising Land Reclamation in Contested Seas for Military Build-up and Operations

The momentum and extent of land reclamation undertaken by China around rock reefs in the South China Sea's Spratly Islands have caused strategic reverberations across Asia. Beijing has managed to construct an artificial island in the South China Sea over the course of 2014 and is continuing even now. The Fiery Cross Reef (part of the Spratly Islands) that was virtually untouched by man-made structures until March 2014 was transformed into an artificial island in exactly a year's time (March 2015). Satellite images revealed that the first section of this artificial creation has a landing strip, and the 3-km runway constructed by China can be put to use for out-and-out military operations. Additionally, building work in the nearby Subi Reef could potentially create space for yet another 3-km airstrip. More recent aerial surveillance images further show a flotilla of Chinese vessels tasked with land-dredging activities, creating ports and battlements in the region – amounting to it becoming, perhaps, the biggest reclamation project – a reported 800 hectares of submerged reef converted into dry land. Accentuating this, the Japanese Foreign Ministry released video footage highlighting Beijing's massive dredging and land reclamation operations in the disputed Spratly Islands as well as footage of a clash between what appeared to be a China Coast Guard vessel and a Vietnamese ship.

While there are concerns in the international community about attempts to unilaterally change the status quo at sea, Japan has been providing seamless support, combining ODA (Official Development Assistance), defence equipment cooperation and capacity-building to help improve sea protection capabilities while calling for strict adherence to the principles of the rule of law.[91] These perilous developments are undoubtedly a blatant and provocative move by China to unilaterally alter the status quo in the area and shall radically alter the regional balance of military power. The energy-rich sea lanes in the South China Sea, through which more than £3.3 trillion worth of trade passes annually, will become more susceptible in the eventuality of this artificial island being converted by China into a full-fledged military base. China has repeatedly defended its "right to establish military facilities on its sovereign territories" and circumvents the issue to "Chinese sovereignty" — much in sync with President Xi Jinping's affirmation of remaining "... strongly committed to safeguarding the country's sovereignty and defending territorial integrity".

The island-reclamation projects in the South China Sea are part of an effort to create core infrastructure for the declaration and enforcement of such a zone within the next several years – thus, making a Chinese ADIZ in the South China Sea a near certainty. A day after the US Department of Defence stated on-record that the US will not recognise an ADIZ in the South China Sea, the Chinese government's spokesperson countered it on April 01, 2016, by saying that if an ADIZ is established in the South China Sea, "it is within China's right" to do so.[92] An ADIZ attempts to push US and allied forces away from Chinese "near seas" and areas of "core interest," while attempting to negate operational concepts such as air sea battle and associated weapons platforms that could challenge China's A2/AD. Declaring an ADIZ is part of a long-term strategy to monitor and restrict foreign military activity (including air intelligence-gathering and radar tracking) in what China describes as its "near seas" – and neutralise the United States' and Japanese efforts to ensure access to the East China Sea.[93]

China is expanding its access to foreign ports to pre-position the necessary logistics support to regularise and sustain deployments in the "far seas" waters as distant as the Indian Ocean, Mediterranean Sea, and Atlantic Ocean. This reflects and amplifies China's growing geo-political clout, extending the reach of its influence and armed forces. The expanding strategic naval footprint in the Indian Ocean by means of acquiring more maritime bases and berthing facilities is a core pillar of China's ports policy. The PLAN's presence and deployment in the IOR have been on the rise since 2014, when a Song-class conventional submarine docked in Colombo harbour along with a Ming-class diesel-electric nuclear submarine. Striking was the fact that the submarine docked at Colombo's South Container Terminal that is built, run, and controlled by China Merchants Holdings — thereby raising queries as to why it did not choose to dock at the Sri Lanka Port Authority in Colombo, which is mandated to accommodate foreign military vessels? The emphasis to dock at a minuscule "Chinese facility" well within a Sri Lankan administered harbour, merits careful analysis. Given its strategic placement, Sri Lanka is fast becoming the pivot of rising Chinese naval presence in the Indian Ocean Region (IOR), in that, China also has a substantial controlling stake in the Hambantota port, with Colombo agreeing to grant

Chinese state-owned companies operating rights to as many as four berths in exchange for an easing of loan conditions. Besides, there were unconfirmed reports of construction of a Chinese-run aircraft maintenance facility near Hambantota in order to service PLAAF assets based in Sri Lanka. In neighbouring Pakistan, the docking of a Chinese submarine in Karachi, following the handing over of the port's operational control to China Overseas Port Holdings is another step towards consolidating a permanent Chinese naval presence in South Asia.[94] These developments, significantly, are in sync with China's much pronounced Maritime Silk Route strategy — a prominent feature of the on-going 13th Five-Year Plan (2016-2020). The maritime route is a proposed sea network of ports, coastal infrastructure projects beginning in Quanzhou in the Fujian province and culminating in the northern Mediterranean Sea. By virtue of this fresh strategy, Beijing seeks to gain greater access to the strategic pathways of the Indian Ocean, and alleviated access to the Gulf oil — which, consequently, shall reduce its dependence on the passage through the Strait of Malacca — a key potential vulnerability for China in the event of a future conflict.

French Defence Minister Jean-Yves Le Drian stated recently that if UNCLOS is openly flouted in the South China Sea, "... it will be in jeopardy in the Arctic, the Mediterranean, and elsewhere tomorrow." Placing this in reference to the recent developments in the IOR, China has sent 21 naval contingencies to the IOR since 2008, with an overt and publicly stated objective of countering piracy, however, projecting power in the region has been an inherently couched aim, as evidenced by the amphibious operations, air defence roles, testing its military-civilian dual use capabilities, and submarine visits. China recognises fully well that in order to boost its naval power projection capability, it will have to gain greater access to ports and berthing facilities. This is being increasingly reflected with China's covert strategy of granting huge loans to smaller coastal island nations that are in dire need of developmental funds to improve infrastructure. The pattern that China is following is almost unvarying, for handing out these loans – with "no conditions and/ or transparency measures" while issuing the loan. As soon as the island nation in question reaches the stage where it is unable to repay the loan on time, China thereafter "offers" to "waive off/relax" loan conditions in exchange for a "few berths" in that particular naval facility. The Maldivian project is a case in point, in which China is developing the iHavan Integrated Development Project in the northernmost main sea line of communication joining Southeast Asia and China to West Asia and Europe. The iHavan project is riding on huge concessional loans/aid financing from China and it is being forecast that Maldives shall almost certainly default on payments, thereby allowing China to seize a few berthing facilities there.[95]

This pattern could well be adopted in the future with many other countries, especially since official Chinese publications including *Xinhua* have advocated and "advised" the PLA Navy to build around 18 overseas naval military bases in the greater Indian Ocean area, possibly including: Chongjin port (North Korea), Moresby port (Papua New Guinea), Sihanoukville port (Cambodia), Koh Lanta port (Thailand), Sittwe port (Myanmar), Dhaka port (Bangladesh), Gwadar port (Pakistan), Hambantota port (Sri Lanka), Maldives, Seychelles, Djibouti port (Djibouti), Lagos port (Nigeria), Mombasa port (Kenya), Dar-es-Salaam port (Tanzania), Luanda port (Angola) and the Walvis Bay port (Namibia). The long shadow of China's ports policy in the Indian Ocean being currently driven and characterised by both state- and private-sponsored "infrastructure investment", foretells strategic ramifications militarily as these facilities shall end up becoming communication and surveillance facilities, in addition to being repair and replenishment centres for the Chinese Navy—underscoring the intransigent course of Beijing's influence in South Asia and the Indian Ocean.[96]

Notwithstanding that China's current naval logistics footprint in the Indian Ocean is unable to support major combat operations in South Asia, China has confirmed building its first overseas "logistics base" for warships in the East African nation of Djibouti, strategically placed between the Indian Ocean and the Red Sea. Scheduled to be complete in 2017, the base is set to resupply Chinese naval warships and sustain the PLAN's operations.[97] The Chinese presence in Djibouti clearly indicates that the Chinese military is expanding beyond its immediate and extended periphery. A "logistics facility" represents an arrangement in which China leases out portions of a commercial port solely for PLAN logistics operations. Such a logistics presence may support both civilian and military operations. The facility in Djibouti notwithstanding, China has not constructed US-styled overseas military bases in the Indian Ocean. China's leaders could well judge instead that a mixture of preferred access to overseas commercial ports and a limited number of exclusive PLAN logistic facilities—probably collocated with commercial ports—most closely aligns with China's future overseas logistics needs to support its evolving naval requirements. Preferred access would give the PLAN favoured status in using a commercial port for resupply, replenishment, and maintenance purposes.[98] The PLAN's goal over the coming decades is slated to being recognised as a stronger regional force able to project power across the greater Asia-Pacific region for high-intensity operations over a sustained period of time. However, the Pentagon has evaluated that logistics and intelligence support continue to remain key obstacles, particularly in the Indian Ocean and in other areas outside the greater Asia-Pacific region. As a result, China desires expansion of its access to logistics in the Indian Ocean and will probably establish several access points in this area in the next decade.

US' National Security Strategy and Joint Operational Access Concept

In response to China's growing movement and presence, both in the maritime zone and air space, the United States began working on a new operational concept known as the Air Sea Battle (ASB) and Joint Operational Access Concept. Designed to attack-in-depth with integrated operations across the air, land, sea, space, and cyber space domains, the ASB is not a strategy. It is an important component of the DoD's strategic mission to project power and sustain operations in the global commons during peace-time or in a crisis.[99] In addition, the Joint Operational Access Concept advocates a concept for joint forces to achieve operational access in the face of armed opposition. It may be noted here that operational access is the ability to project military force into an operational area with sufficient freedom of action to accomplish broader strategic goals. China's A2/AD capabilities are challenging the ability to ensure operational access – and may well be the most difficult operational challenge that the US forces are likely to face in the coming decades. The US forces seek to conduct operations to gain access by preparing the operational area in advance to facilitate access and follow it up by disrupting or destroying the adversary's anti-access/area-denial capabilities/defences in depth rather than rolling back those defences from the perimeter.[100] The core of the US military's Air Sea Battle concept seeks to better integrate the Services, aimed at enhancing US power projection – expected to serve as a key support component of the US National Security Strategy (NSS) for the 21st century – released in February 2015 by President Barack Obama. It is only pertinent to mention here that the 2015 US NSS document came five years after 2010 when it was last published. The document hinges fundamentally on strengthening the foundations of America's power – political, economic, and military — and sustains American leadership in the new century. Just like the previous document in 2010, this one too, emphasises on a strategy guided by security and a rules-based international order among other things. In the midst of the growing debate surrounding the American leadership in the 21st century, Washington has renewed its core alliances and is simultaneously rebalancing to the regions that will do more to determine the course of the 21st century, with East Asia, being a prime one among them. The US' rebalance, starting with the Asia-Pacific, is deepening long-standing alliances, while simultaneously forging new partnerships to expand cooperation. Washington has been investing in ASEAN, the East Asia Summit, and the Pacific Islands Forum to strengthen capacities to enforce regional norms, and resolve disputes peacefully, so that the Asia-Pacific remains a region that projects dynamic growth and opportunity. US National Security Adviser Susan Rice accepted that with China, the US is building a constructive relationship that expands practical cooperation, even as the two confront real differences over the use of coercion to advance territorial claims.[101]

The Air Sea Battle Concept

At its core, the Air Sea Battle (ASB) concept is about reducing risk and maintaining freedom and space for action to improve US capabilities – thus, constituting a key part of US national security strategy for the 21st century. The ASB is a limited, yet critical component in a spectrum of initiatives during peace-time or a crisis, and the term was first coined in a 1992 paper by then-Commander of the US National War College, James Stavridis, calling for new ways of organising airborne and seaborne forces. The ASB received official endorsement in the 2010 US *Quadrennial Defense Review*, which called upon the Air Force and Navy to develop:

> [A] new joint air-sea battle concept for defeating adversaries across the range of military operations, including adversaries equipped with sophisticated anti-access and area denial capabilities. The concept will address how air and naval forces will integrate capabilities across all operational domains—air, sea, land, space, and cyber space—to counter growing challenges to US freedom of action.[102]

The ASB concept supports the Joint Operational Access Concept (JOAC), and is not an operational plan or strategy for a specific region/adversary. The purpose of ASB is not just conducting operations jointly, but increasing operational advantage across all domains, enhancing Service capabilities and mitigating vulnerabilities. Specifically in the Asia-Pacific, there is no denying that ASB is the pivot of the United States Pacific Command (USPACOM) operations and A2/AD counter-warfare. The ASB is a derivative of the Air Land Battle concept developed in the 1970s and 1980s to counter a Soviet-backed combined arms attack in Europe. A key component of Air Land Battle was the degradation of rear echelon forces before they could engage allied forces – with the mission being assigned majorly to the Air Force, to be further coordinated with the Army.

In July 2009, the US Secretary of Defence directed the Departments of the Navy and the Air Force to address the A2/AD challenge and embark on a new operational concept called Air Sea Battle. Since then, the US Army, Marine Corps, Navy, and Air Force have collaborated in innovative ways. In the Fall of 2012, all four of the Services' Vice Chiefs signed a memorandum of understanding establishing a framework to implement the ASB concept through the development of a joint force capable of shaping and exploiting A2/AD environments to maintain freedom of action in the global commons, and secure operational access to enable concurrent or follow on joint operations. Cyber space and space-based capabilities are essential for US operations and stand vulnerable to the adversary's capabilities with a low barrier to entry such as computer network attack and electronic jamming. Besides, capabilities such as ballistic and cruise missiles will be used with ambiguous or minimal warning, requiring

US and Japanese forces to be routinely integrated and prepared to conduct high-risk operations. At the low end of the conflict spectrum, Air Sea Battle enables conducting a show of force or initiating limited strikes, and engaging with partners to assure access to international waters and air space. Further, at the high end of the conflict spectrum, it preserves the ability to maintain escalation advantage during conflict and sustaining security despite the presence of advanced weapon systems of the adversary.[103]

Designed to attack-in-depth (i.e., force projection through denied space zones), the ASB is designed to integrate networked operations across all five interdependent war-fighting domains (air, maritime, land, space, and cyber space) to Disrupt, Destroy, and Defeat (D3) the A2/AD capabilities and provide maximum operational advantage to the US and its allies/partners, with three lines of effort:

- Disrupt/the adversary's Command, Control, Communications, Computers, Intelligence, Surveillance, and Reconnaissance (C4ISR or C4I);
- Destroy/adversary's A2/AD platforms and weapons launchers including missile sites, aircrafts, ships; and,
- Defeat/adversary's active employed weapons and formations (located in any warfare domain, in order to gain access to the theatre.[104]

The *Air Sea Battle: Service Collaboration to Address Anti-Access and Area Denial Challenges* (version 9) published in May 2013 argues in favour of distributed control, which mitigates risk associated with over-centralisation; empowers lower-echelon Commanders, and increases flexibility; organises bases or carrier battle groups into clusters under a single Commander, based on the ability to reach back to the AOC; and provides forward C2. The numerous assets with the Services that are available to enable forward C2, include the E-3 Airborne Warning and Control System (AWACS), E-2 Hawkeye, E-8 Joint Surveillance Target Attack Radar System (JSTARS), RC-135 Rivet Joint, control and reporting centres, Aegis cruisers, and others. Ultimately, layers of distributed control lead to enhanced survivability and flexibility, leaving the adversary unable to render US fielded forces crippled with a single, decisive blow.[105] RAdm James G. Foggo III, then chair of the Air Sea Battle Senior Steering Group, gave perhaps the most lucid public description in a testimony in October 2013 before the Subcommittee for Seapower and Projection Forces of the US Senate Armed Services Committee, in which he clearly defined the ASB concept, clarifying that it is no strategy, but, in fact, an operational military concept:[106]

> ... The (ASB) is designed to assure access to parts of the "global commons"—those areas of the air, sea, cyberspace and space that no one "owns," but which we all depend on—such as the sea lines of communication. Our adversaries' anti-access/ area denial strategies employ a range of military capabilities that impede the free use of these

> ungoverned spaces. These military capabilities include new generations of cruise, ballistic, air-to-air, and surface-to-air missiles with improved range, accuracy, and lethality [which] are being produced and proliferated...Accordingly, the Air Sea Battle Concept is intended to defeat such threats to access.[107]

Deterrence by Denial

The consistent critique of the ASB has been that deep strikes on China would be excessively escalatory or counter-productive, lacking credibility to deter a limited, small-scale conflict in the East China Sea or South China Sea. In the light of this critique, several alternatives were introduced, with *Deterrence By Denial* (DBD) becoming a prominent one – first proposed as a strategy by Andrew Erickson at the US Naval War College in December 2013. In a statement before the Senate Armed Services Committee on Seapower and Projection Forces,[108] Erickson argued that the United States must ensure that its security commitments in the Asia-Pacific are not hollowed out by China's ability to threaten both its neighbours and Washington. Instead of focussing on deterrence through punishment, as ASB does, an approach emphasising *deterrence through denial* would be more effective in preventing China's likely expansionist goals. In attempting to seize islands in the East or South China Seas, Beijing's forces would be operating in an offence-dominated environment, which would be prone to a volatile turnaround if another nation wanted to challenge its gains.[109] Therefore, in order for the US and its regional allies to maximise their own disruption capabilities through bolstered A2/AD defences, DBD proposes that they invest in, and deploy, as quickly as possible, certain high pay-off military capabilities.[110] These include advanced surface-to-surface, air-to-surface, and surface-to-air missiles, in addition to extra naval mines and submarines.[111] By building on such capabilities, Erickson asserts, "US submarines can oppose any Chinese naval forces engaged in invasion, resupply, and protection. Long-range air or missile delivery can blow any lodgement off disputed islands or rocks."[112]

In this backdrop, would China exercise the so-called "first-mover advantage" by building on strategic offence combined with tactical defence, entailing Beijing to preempt its opponents by taking the Senkaku Islands, thereby forcing Japan to reclaim them? Beijing's hardball approach to the East China Sea is the gradualist model of expansion, geared toward creating a *de facto* sphere of influence in the East China Sea. Alternatively, will China attempt to seize another set of disputed islands in a military operation without actual combat? It should be recalled that Beijing did accomplish such a feat in 2012 when it seized control of the Scarborough Shoal from the Philippines by using only Coast Guard vessels.[113] In April 2012, government vessels from both nations faced off for several weeks at the Scarborough Shoal with the Chinese military effectively seizing control of the Scarborough Shoal in the South China Sea later in July 2012 from the Philippines without having to resort to war. Having found success in redefining the status quo in the above scenario, the Chinese leadership appears heavily inclined toward upstaging the rule-based international order and altering the status quo in its favour with respect to regional disputes with Japan over the Senkaku Islands.[114]

However, a larger operation, for instance, the attempted seizure of the Senkaku Islands from Japan, would pose a far greater challenge for China. In the case of Chinese maritime aggression, *deterrence by denial*, proposes to neutralise Chinese troops and their logistical chain by relying particularly on America's undersea advantages. It can be interpreted as a small-scale approach to prevent Chinese aggression over islands in the East China Sea – being a flexible approach that covers the entire spectrum of escalation responses. The theory of conflict termination in reference to deterrence by denial would be strengthened by the fact that, if China decided to intensify the conflict, the United States will respond with a debilitating blockade.[115]

Joint Concept for Access and Manoeuvre in the Global Commons

The ASB has been renamed by the Pentagon as the *Joint Concept for Access and Manoeuvre in the Global Commons* (JAM-GC). According to media reports in January 2015, an internal memo obtained by *USNI*

News, the Air Sea Battle Office (ASBO) was integrated into the Joint Staff J-7 Directorate (Joint Force Development), tasked to "monitor and support development of JAM-GC as required." With a high possibility of massive conventional strikes on China's mainland to take out its systems through force, the actual war plans of the JAM-GC remain classified. However, it has been reported that the JAM-GC has been put to test in numerous war games and integrated into the Pentagon's planning for usage in contested operating environments. In an article for *The National Interest*, experts from the Air Sea Battle Office at the Pentagon laid out a vision for what Air Sea Battle will become:

> An updated supporting joint concept will also describe an evolutionary approach to joint and allied operations across Service, component and multinational lines in A2/AD environments. Building on existing JOAC precepts, the refined concept will incorporate the most useful ideas from the existing 'ASB Concept' ...Based on recent assessments, current doctrinal command-and-control methodologies will likely be inadequate to address A2/AD environments where beyond line-of-sight communications and other connectivity between units can be disrupted or denied by an adversary. Therefore, evolutionary modifications to command-and-control structures and protocols are necessary in order to effectively command and control

> Joint Forces in a heavily disrupted electromagnetic-spectrum environment. Additionally, cross-domain expertise within component and lower-echelon operations centers must be leveraged to create cross-domain effects in support of the commanders' intent and schemes of maneuver.[116]

Simultaneously, Japan too, has begun work on parallel concepts such as "dynamic defence", which can be termed as part of an overall strategy of efficient deterrence and response. In fact, Japan's new National Defence Programme Guidelines (NDPG) call for the building of a Dynamic Joint Defence Force, in place of the Dynamic Defence Force from the 2010 NDPG, as the cornerstone for the protection of Japan's peace and security. The new NDPG, calls for the enhancement of deterrent and response capabilities by pursuing further joint operations, improving the operational standards of defence equipment, and further increasing defence activities. The new NDPG, for the first time, implemented the capability assessment based on a joint operation regarding various anticipated circumstances – a sufficient level of "quality" and "quantity" of the defence force will be required in order to build effective deterrence, particularly in the present security environment; ensuring maritime supremacy and air superiority; ensuring the "quality" and "quantity" of the defence force by focussing on developing the mobile deployment capability; strengthening a wide range of logistical support foundations in order to perform a variety of activities effectively. The new NDPG stands firmly footed on the recognition that Japan-US Security Arrangements contribute to stability in the Asia-Pacific region. Japan will revise the Guidelines for Japan-US Defence Cooperation, further enhance Japan-US defence cooperation and reinforce the deterrence provided by the Japan-US alliance and the alliance's contingency response capabilities.[117] Japan-US cooperation is being redefined especially in response to "grey zone" situations – which are neither peace-time, nor unforeseen events, calling for emergency response mechanisms. These "grey zone" incidents need not necessarily involve a military attack or surge, but surely would be in the midst of rising military tensions. And further could be contextualised in the given situation as an attempt to forcefully occupy a remote islet/island. To that end, Japan will expand joint training and exercises, joint Intelligence, Surveillance, and Reconnaissance (ISR) activities and the joint/shared use of facilities and areas with the US. More specifically, the scope of the role of the SDF shall now be expanded, in line with the Japanese government's new interpretation of the Constitution, which allows the SDF to protect US vessels under armed attacks in grey zone situations, in addition to enabling the nation to exercise, within a limited range, the right of collective self-defence.

Moreover, the Maritime Self-Defence Force (MSDF) has apparently increased the number of Japanese destroyers from 48 in the 2010 NDPG (12 escort divisions) to 54 (14 escort divisions) by using new destroyers that offer improved response capabilities for various missions and have more compact designs and will maintain ship-based patrol helicopter units in order to secure the defence of surrounding waters and ensure the safety of maritime traffic. Besides, two Aegis-equipped destroyers will be added, bringing the fleet to eight. The MSDF patrols the waters surrounding Hokkaido, the Sea of Japan, and the East China Sea in peace-time, using P-3C and other patrol aircraft to monitor the numerous vessels that sail through those waters. In 2013, for example, there were eight incidents of activity by Chinese Navy vessels involving the passage through the southwestern region and four incidents of such activity were also confirmed in waters south of Okinawa. Moreover, since the Japanese government's acquisition of the ownership of the Senkaku Islands in September 2012, Chinese governmental ships have intermittently intruded into Japanese territorial waters. The Japan Coast Guard too, has strengthened its warning and surveillance activities through the use of patrol ships and aircraft, and demanded that the Chinese ships that intruded into Japanese territorial waters surrounding the Senkaku Islands leave.

The Japanese Air Self-Defence Force (ASDF) will maintain air warning and control units in order to provide persistent ISR in most air space over Japan and the surrounding areas. By consolidating warning and control operations at air defence command centres, the ASDF will gradually change warning groups into warning squadrons as well as establish one new squadron in the air-warning unit. As for Fighter Aircraft Units, the 13th squadron will be newly established, and the Air Reconnaissance Unit will be abolished. In addition, one squadron will be added to the Aerial Refuelling/Transport Unit, making it a two-squadron architecture. The ASDF will maintain surface-to-air guided missile units providing multi-layered defence for Japan against ballistic missile attacks, together with the Aegis destroyers, as well as protecting key areas in tandem with the surface-to-air guided missile units of the GSDF. The MSDF patrols the waters surrounding Hokkaido, the Sea of Japan, and the East China Sea in peace-time, using P-3C and other patrol aircraft to monitor the numerous vessels that sail through those waters. The ASDF uses radar sites at 28 locations nationwide, E-2C early warning aircraft, and E-767 early warning and control aircraft, amongst others, to carry out warning and surveillance activities over Japan and its surrounding air space round the clock.

Under international law, nations have complete and exclusive sovereignty over their air space. Scrambling against intruding aircraft takes place to exercise the right of policing intended to maintain public order. Unlike measures taken on land or in the seas, this measure can be taken only by the SDF. Therefore, the ASDF is primarily responsible for conducting actions against intruding aircraft based on Article 84 of the SDF Act, promptly and seamlessly. Even after the establishment of the East China Sea Air Defence Identification Zone by China, the MoD and the SDF have been implementing surveillance activities as before, in the East China Sea, including the zone in question, and have continued to take all initiatives necessary to engage in surveillance in the sea and air space around Japan. The Ministry of Defence defines the ADIZ in the area surrounding Japan in order to identify aircraft flying around Japan by using radar and takes effective counter-measures against intrusions into Japanese air space. China's naval build-up and its supposed goal of building a submarine base in the Senkaku region greatly concern Tokyo. The Japanese are further concerned that the Chinese have expanded their defences and defence perimeters farther from the coast and are approaching areas that are sensitive to Japanese national security. Numerous commentaries on Chinese claims in the East and South China Seas published in recent years in state-controlled Chinese media have issued repeated veiled warnings that "... with increased comprehensive national strength, China will use more effective ways". This vindicates the argument that has been long-standing that as much as China bawls for what it describes as "peaceful" rise, coupled with incessant banality that China "will never seek hegemony", it is only verified on the contrary that the Chinese rise, both economically and militarily, backed by its political leadership, constantly attempts to create a fresh status quo in all its existing territorial disputes, on both land, and at sea.

It has often been suggested that a viable and attractive alternative for managing Sino-Japanese strategic relations is to design a multilateral mechanism for promoting bilateral cooperation. This is because the motion of relative gains (or losses) becomes ambiguous with more than two players, whereas Japan and China, under a bilateral framework, are likely to define their mutual relations by the logic of zero-sum games in which cooperation is not viable. In order to achieve relative gains collectively versus others, Japan and China have separately embarked on seeking "defensive cooperation" with their own allies or like-minded partners.[118] A palpable outcome is that bilateral relations will suffer from continuing tensions given that currently very few institutionalised cooperative structures deal effectively with security issues in the region.[119] In the long term, trust and confidence-building may be one of the results of cooperation in building crisis communication mechanisms, and eventually create a situation in which the focus shifts to crisis prevention, which will lead to real long-term gains in regional stability and security in the East China Sea.[120]

China's relations with its neighbours perhaps are at their worse with Beijing's provocative and cantankerous actions, especially in the East Asian waters and elsewhere, and the move of announcing the ADIZ has made matters worse. What comes across unambiguously is that the Chinese leadership under Xi Jinping is firmly backing the Chinese antagonistic moves in the East China Sea and the South China Sea. The Xi administration seems heavily inclined towards testing the tenacity and credibility of the security alliances in the Asia-Pacific region, including the US' equation with Japan and the Philippines. While Japan has declined backing down, with Japan's Foreign Minister Fumio Kishida refusing to recognise China's claimed air defence identification zone over the Senkaku Islands, former US Secretary of Defence Chuck Hagel viewed the Chinese move as a "destabilising attempt to alter the status quo in the region" and reaffirmed Washington's longstanding policy under Article V of the US-Japan Mutual Defence Treaty which applies to the Senkaku Islands—given that the US acknowledges Japan's administrative control over the Senkaku Islands. Covering wide areas of the East China Sea between South Korea and Taiwan, critically including the Senkaku islets, Chinese activity remains an attempt to strengthen its claims while strategising offensive posturing vis-à-vis the Senkaku Islands. It is a surreptitious attempt to affirm control by insisting that there, indeed, is a dispute over the Senkaku Islands and providing a platform for the long-term Chinese strategy of chipping away at Japanese claims.

Notes

1. Haruko Satoh, "Japan: What Future with China?" in *East Asia's Relations with a Rising China*, published by Konrad Adenauer Stiftung, p. 201.
2. For more details, see TJ Christensen, "China, the US-Japan Alliance, and the Security Dilemma in East Asia," in GJ Ikenberry and M

Mastanduno, eds., *International Relations Theory and the Asia-Pacific* (New York: Columbia University Press, 2003).

3. Krista E Wiegand, "China's Strategy in the Senkaku/Diaoyu Islands Dispute: Issue Linkage and Coercive Diplomacy," *Asian Security*, Vol. 5, No. 2, 2009, pp. 170-193.
4. Alexander L. George and William E. Simons, eds., *The Limits of Coercive Diplomacy* (Boulder: Westview Press, 1994), p. 10, cited in Wiegand, Ibid.
5. Alexander George, *Forceful Persuasion: Coercive Diplomacy as an Alternative to War* (Washington, DC: United States Institute of Peace Press, 1991), p. 11.
6. David W. Leeborn, "Linkages," *The American Journal of International Law,* Vol. 96, No. 1, 2002, pp. 5-27; also see Robert O. Keohane and Joseph Nye, *Power and Interdependence,*(Boston: Little, Brown and Company, 1977).
7. Wiegand, n. 3.
8. Paul J Smith, "China-Japan Relations and the Future Geopolitics of East Asia," *Asian Affairs: An American Review*, Vol. 35, No. 4, 2009.
9. Wang Jian Wei, "The US-Japan Alliance in the 21st Century: A Chinese Perspective" in Purnendra Jain and Lam Peng Er, eds., *Japan's Strategic Challenges in a Changing Regional Environment* (MA: World Scientific Publishing Co. Pvt. Ltd., 2013), pp. 28-29.
10. Ibid.
11. Tetsuo Kotani, "Turbulent Changes: The Democratic Party Government and Japan's Foreign Policy", *Russia in Global Affairs*, Vol. 8, No. 4, December 2010; and see Daniel Sneider, "The New Asianism: Japanese Foreign Policy under the Democratic Party of Japan", *Asia Policy*, No. 12, July 2011.
12. For more on Hatoyama's 'mismanagement of the alliance' see, Kotani, Ibid.
13. "Ozawa-led Group Welcomed in China/Hu, DPJ Officials Look", *The Yomiuri Shimbun*, December 12, 2009.
14. "Yan Jiechi's Visit to Japan: China-Japan Relations Redefined," www.sohu.com, November 21, 2009.

15. Wang Lihuan, "The post-Cold War China-ASEAN and Japan ASEAN Relations," *Science of International Politics*, No. 3, 2006, pp. 56-63.
16. He Yingying, "The Evolution of Japan's East Asian Regionalism and its Influence on the Regional Strategy of Economic Cooperation," *Collection of Japanese Studies*, June 2007, p. 6.
17. Toshio Nishi, "The New Japanese Nationalism", article published by The Hoover Institution, December 19, 2012; according to an opinion poll conducted by *Jiji Press* in January 2013, 56.7 per cent of those surveyed thought Shinzo Abe should visit the Yasukuni Shrine, up from 43 per cent in 2006.
18. "Dangerous Waters: China-Japan Relations on the Rocks," *Asia Report*, No. 245, *International Crisis Group Publication*, April 2013, Beijing/Brussels.
19. "Abe Stresses Resolve to Defend Senkakus" *Jiji Press*, January 12, 2013.
20. Paul O'Shea, "Sovereignty and the Senkaku/Diaoyu Territorial Dispute," Stockholm School of Economics, *Working Paper*, No. 240, September 2012.
21. Ibid.
22. Ibid.
23. For more details, see Alexander Wendt, "Anarchy is what States Make of it: The Social Construction of Power Politics," *International Organization,* Vol. 46, No. 2, 1992, pp. 391-425.
24. For more details, see Janice E. Thomson, "State Sovereignty in International Relations: Bridging the Gap between Theory and Empirical Research," *International Studies Quarterly,* Vol. 39, No. 2, 1995, pp. 213-33.
25. "Congress Elects Yang Jing, Chang Wanquan, Yang Jiechi, Guo Shengkun and Wang Yong State Councilors," *Xinhua News Agency*, March 16, 2013; also see n. 18.
26. David Lampton, "China's Foreign and National Security Policy-making Process: Is it Changing, and Does it Matter?" in David Lampton, ed., *The Making of Chinese Foreign and Security Policy,* (Stanford, 2001), pp. 1-36.
27. For more details and on the larger debate on China-Japan relations,

see Ming Wan, *Understanding Japan-China Relations: Theories and Issues* (World Scientific Publishing Company, 2015); more specifically on the China school, see Masahiko Sasajima, "Japan's Domestic Politics and China Policymaking" in Benjamin L. Self and Jeffrey W. Thomson eds., *An Alliance for Engagement: Building Cooperation in Security Relations with China* (Washington D.C., 2002), p. 83.

28. n. 18.
29. *The US-Japan Alliance to 2030: Power and Principle,* Bilateral Commission Report 2013, by the Sasakawa Peace Foundation and Center for Strategic and International Studies (Co-chaired by Richard Armitage, John Hamre, and Ryozo Kato) with an objective to develop a shared vision for Asia.
30. For more details and reference, see Katahara Eiichi, "Japan's Strategic Options?" in Jain and Er, n. 9, pp. 3-4.
31. R Jade Harry, "A Solution Acceptable to All? A Legal Analysis of the Senkaku-Diaoyu Island Dispute," *Cornell International Law Journal*, Vol. 46, No. 653, 2013.
32. Ibid.
33. Ibid.
34. Ibid.
35. For more details, see M Taylor Fravel, "Explaining Stability in the Senkaku (Diaoyu) Dispute," in Gerald Curtis, Ryosei Kokubun and Wang Jisi, eds., *Getting the Triangle Straight: Managing China-Japan-US Relations* (Washington, DC: The Brookings Institution Press, 2010).
36. *Senkaku (Diaoyu/Diaoyutai) Islands Dispute: US Treaty Obligations*, Congressional Research Service Report, January 22, 2013.
37. Akira Kato, "The United States: The Hidden Actor in the Senkaku Islands," *Asia Pacific Bulletin*, East West Center, No. 205, April 02, 2013.
38. Christian Le Mière, "Rebalancing the Burden in East Asia," *Survival*, Vol. 55, No. 2, April-May 2013, pp. 31-41; and see Martin Fackler, "Cautiously, Japan Raises Military Profile as China Rises," *The New*

York Times, November 26, 2012; also see "Japan Aims to Revise Pact with US: Defense Minister Wants Alliance to Consider Risk of a Sea Clash with China", *The International Herald Tribune,* November 01, 2012.

39. Eiichi, n. 30, p. 21.
40. Annual Report to Congress, *Military and Security Developments involving the People's Republic of China 2016,* Office of the Secretary of Defense; Section 1246, "Annual Report on Military and Security Developments Involving the People's Republic of China," of the National Defense Authorization Act for Fiscal Year 2010, Public Law 111-84, which amends the National Defense Authorization Act for Fiscal Year 2000, Section 1202, Public Law 106-65, provides that the Secretary of Defense shall submit a report in both classified and unclassified form, on military and security developments involving the People's Republic of China. Hereafter referred to as the DoD *China Report* 2016.
41. Ibid.
42. Eiichi, n. 30, pp. 4-5.
43. Feng Liang, *Zhongguo de Hepingfazhan yu Haishang Anquan Huanjing* ["China's Peaceful Development and Maritime Security Environment] (Beijing: Shijie Zhishi Chubanshe, 2010), p. 184.
44. Xu Qi, "Maritime Geo-strategy and the Development of the Chinese Navy in the Early Twenty-First Century," *Naval War College Review*, Vol. 56, No. 4, Autumn 2006.
45. Sun Yat-Sen, leader of the Chinese Nationalist Party (Kuomintang), known as the father of modern China, was influential in overthrowing the Qing (Manchu) dynasty and thereafter served as the first provisional president of the Republic of China (1911-12).
46. Chu Shulong, "The Current Situation in Remote Chinese Territorial Waters and its External Strategic Design," *Xiandai Guoji Guanxi*, No. 8, 2012.
47. Jin Canrong, "The Context and Resolution of Chinese Maritime Territorial Disputes," *Xiandai Guoji Guanxi*, No. 8, 2012.
48. For more details, see the Report by the Asia Centre, European Council on Foreign Relations, "Shockwaves from the China/Japan Island Dispute", February 2013; also see, Peng Guangqian, "If Japan

Fires Tracer Shot, That Would Count as 'Firing the First Shot,'" *People's Daily,* January 14, 2012.

49. For arguments on a qualitative change of China's maritime policy, see Zhang Jie, "*Huangyandao Duizhi yu Zhongguohaishanganquan Zhengce Zhuanxiang*" [Huangyan Island Confrontation and China's Maritime Security Policy Transformation] in Zhang Jie, ed., *Zhongguo Zhoubian Anquan Xingshi Pinggu 2013, China's Regional Security Environment Review* (Shehui Kexue Wenxian Chubanshe, 2013), pp. 54-56.
50. "Japan Extends Military Reach in Disputed East China Sea," *The Guardian*, March 28, 2016.
51. Richard L. Armitage and Joseph S. Nye, "The US-Japan Alliance Anchoring Stability in Asia," A Report of the Center for Strategic and International Studies, Japan Chair, August 2012, pp. 8-9.
52. Takanori Higurashi, *Okinawa wo nerau Chugoku no yashin*, Tokyo, Shodensha, 2009, p. 212.
53. *Diaoyu Dao, an Inherent Territory of China*, White Paper released by the State Council Information Office, People's Republic of China, Beijing, September 2012.
54. Armitage and Nye, n. 51, p. 11.
55. Ibid., p. 12.
56. "Relationship between the Right of Collective Self-Defense and the Constitution", submitted by the Government to the Committee on Audit of the House of Councillors on October 14, 1972.
57. Hu Jintao's report at 18th Party Congress, cited in *People's Daily,* November 19, 2012, available at http://english.people.com.cn/90785/8024777.html
58. n. 40.
59. For more details and references, see Monika Chansoria, *Nuclear China: A Veiled Secret* (New Delhi: KW Publishers Pvt Ltd., 2014), see, also n. 40.
60. Ibid.
61. Ibid.
62. n. 40.
63. Ibid.

64. For related details, see Richard D Fisher Jr, "China Advances Sea- and Land-Based Nuclear Deterrent Capabilities," *IHS Jane's Defence Weekly*, Washington, DC, December 16, 2015.
65. n. 40.
66. Ibid.
67. Ibid.
68. Jan Van Tol et al., *Air-Sea Battle: A Point of Departure Operational Concept* (Washington, DC: Center for Strategic and Budgetary Assessments, 2010), pp. ix-xii.
69. n. 40.
70. Sam J. Tangredi, *Anti-Access Warfare: Countering A2/AD Strategies* (Annapolis: Naval Institute Press, 2013).
71. The Air-Sea Battle Office, "Air-Sea Battle: Services Collaboration to Address Anti-Access & Area Denial Challenges," The Air-Sea Battle Office, May 2013, available at http://www.defense.gov/pubs/ASB-ConceptImplementation-Summary-May-2013.pdf
72. Lyle Goldstein and Shannon Knight, "Wired for Sound in the Near Seas," *USNI Proceedings Magazine*, April 2014.
73. "Air-Sea Battle: Service Collaboration to Address Anti-Access & Area Denial Challenges" [May 2013... Unclassified Summary of the classified Air-Sea Battle Concept, version 9.0, dated May 12 and the Air-Sea Battle Master Implementation Plan (FY 2013)].
74. Andrew F Krepinevich, Jr., "The Pentagon's Wasting Assets: The Eroding Foundations of American Power," *Foreign Affairs*, Vol. 88, No. 4, July-August 2009, pp. 18-33.
75. Sketches of the First Island Chain should, therefore, be viewed with caution; for related details, see Toshi Yoshihara and James Holmes, *Red Star over the Pacific: China's Rise and the Challenge to U.S. Maritime Strategies* (Annapolis: Naval Institute Press, 2010), p. 47.
76. For more details, see *Taiwan's 2009 National Defense Report*.
77. Japanese Annual Defense White Paper, *Defense of Japan 2014*, Ministry of Defense, Tokyo.
78. Toshi Yoshihara's views, cited in Franz-Stefan Gady, "This is Japan's Best Strategy to Defeat China at Sea," *The Diplomat*, February 20, 2015.

79. n. 77.
80. Ji Guoxing, "SLOC Security in the Asia Pacific," *Occasional Paper*, Asia-Pacific Center for Security Studies, Honolulu, Hawaii, February 2000.
81. "Voice: China Should Accelerate Legislation on Overseas Military Operations," Ministry of Defense of the People's Republic of China, cited in, *China Military Online*, March 08, 2016.
82. Based on the author's interview with a Japanese Rear Admiral in Tokyo who spoke on the strict condition of anonymity.
83. n. 77.
84. Ibid.
85. Ibid.
86. Monika Chansoria, "The Rise of an Assertive China," *The Pioneer*, December 15, 2013.
87. Ibid.
88. Ibid.
89. For more details, see Mike Yeo, "US Navy: Growing P-8 Poseidon; Operations in the Western Pacific," *USNI News*, March 02, 2015.
90. Chansoria, n. 86.
91. "Without Naming Names, Japan Video Showcases Effort to Halt China Maritime Expansion," *The Japan Times*, March 15, 2016.
92. "China Defends Right to set up Air Defense Identification Zone," as reported in *GB TIMES*, April 01, 2016.
93. Peter Mattis, "China's East China Sea ADIZ: Framing Japan to Help Washington Understand," *China Brief*, December 05, 2013.
94. Monika Chansoria, "China Eyes 18 Overseas Naval Bases," *The Sunday Guardian*, August 15, 2015.
95. Ibid.
96. Ibid.
97. Dong Zhaohui files a report, "China's Logistic Hub in Djibouti to Stabilize Region, Protect Interests," *Global Times*, March 15, 2016.
98. n. 40.
99. n. 73.
100. *Joint Operational Access Concept* (JOAC), Version 1.0, US Department of Defense, January 17, 2012.

101. Remarks by US National Security Advisor, Susan Rice, *2015 United States National Security Strategy*, Office of the Press Secretary, The White House (For Immediate Release), February 06, 2015.
102. For more details, see Department of Defense, *Quadrennial Defense Review Report, Department of Defense*, February 2010.
103. n. 73.
104. Ibid; additionally, also see Greenert and Schwartz, "Air-Sea Battle: Promoting Stability in an Era of Uncertainty"; and see Eirik Torsvoll Deterring Conflict with China: A Comparison of the Air-Sea Battle Concept, Offshore Control, and Deterrence by Denial," *The Fletcher Forum of World Affairs*, Vol. 39, No. 1, Winter 2015, p. 41.
105. William H. Ballard, Mark C. Harysch, et al., "Operationalizing Air-Sea Battle in the Pacific," *Air and Space Power Journal*, January-February 2015.
106. James G. Foggo III, Testimony before the Senate Armed Services Committee, *Subcommittee for Seapower and Projection Forces*, October 10, 2013, available at https://armedservices.house.gov/; For a full transcript of Foggo's opening statement, see Ronald O'Rourke, "China Naval Modernization: Implications for U.S. Navy Capabilities—Background and Issues for Congress," *Congressional Research Service*, February 28, 2014.
107. US Navy, "Read Admiral Foggo Discusses Air-Sea Battle Concept," *Navy Live*, October 10, 2013.
108. See Andrew S. Erickson, "China's Naval Modernization: Implications and Recommendations," Testimony to the Senate Armed Services Committee, April 2013.
109. Andrew S. Erickson, "Watch This Space: China's New Air Defense Zone," *The Wall Street Journal*, November 25, 2013.
110. Erickson, n. 108.
111. Andrew S. Erickson, "Deterrence by Denial: How to Prevent China from Using Force" *The National Interest*, December 16, 2013; also see Scott C. Truver, "Taking Mines Seriously: Mine Warfare in China's Near Seas," *Naval War College Review*, Vol. 65, No. 2, Spring 2012, pp. 30-66.
112. Erickson, n. 108.

113. M. Taylor Fravel, "China's Island Strategy: Redefine the Status Quo," *The Diplomat*, November 01, 2012.
114. Monika Chansoria, "China-Philippines Face-off Heightens Regional Tension," *The Manila Times*, April 20, 2014.
115. Torsvoll, n. 104, p. 55.
116. Terry S. Morris et al., "Securing Operational Access: Evolving the Air-Sea Battle Concept," *The National Interest*, February 11, 2015.
117. *Initiatives of Defense of Japan* released by the Ministry of Defense, Tokyo, Japan.
118. Yasuhiro Takeda, "Sino-Japanese Strategic Relations in Multilateral Regional Frameworks," in Niklas Swanstrom and Ryosei Kokubun, eds., *Sino-Japanese Relations: Rivals or Partners in Regional Cooperation?* (Singapore: World Scientific Publishing Co. Ltd., 2013).
119. Swanstrom and Kokubun, Ibid., pp. 4-5.
120. Ye Zicheng, *Inside China's Grand Strategy: The Perspective from the People's Republic*, Translated by Steven I Levine and Gouoli Liu, (New Delhi: KW Publishers Pvt Ltd, 2013), pp. 8-9.

6. Reigniting a Quiescent Volcano: Is there a Finish Line to the Dispute over the Senkakus?

> *Deep within, China knows it can never get control of these islands, and, Japan too, has discerned that China, shall never, let go ...*
> *And this, essentially, constitutes, and describes, the fabric of the Sino-Japanese relationship, casting a shadow on the overall East Asian security architecture ...*

Detrimental historical legacies have weighed down major inter-state relationships in Asia. China's increasingly aggressive territorial and maritime claims, which have become so evident in the recent few years, underscore the bitter historical legacy as Asia becomes politically more divided. The security dilemma illustrates the acrimonious past between China and Japan that will continue to be the most intractable subject in their bilateral relationship, which undeniably shall have profound ramifications in the larger East Asian regional context. The Senkaku/Diaoyu Islands dispute entails complex overlapping thematic aspects which include territorial integrity, maritime defence space, the Japan-US alliance, economic interests, oil, gas, fishing, seabed resources, international law requirements, domestic circumstances flaming political instability, the rise of non-governmental actors, national identity issues and historical grievances. As a natural consequence, this raises the question of whether any further worsening of the Sino-Japanese relationship shall accord some sort of permanence to the long-simmering dispute over the Senkakus in terms of history, legal implications, and strategic, symbolic, and economic value, and the underlying debate over their sovereignty? This query becomes far more pronounced in the backdrop of a potential eventuality of the islands becoming a time bomb that could explode with an unexpected ignition – not just impacting the future stability between Japan and China, but that of entire East Asia and the global powers directly involved in the region.

Normative Debates on Security and Alliances in East Asia

Japan is a country where the rule of law prevails and separation of powers is the basic structure of the system. However, China does not share this system and in none of its disputes with neighbouring countries has China staked a territorial claim on the basis of international law or norms. Rather, its claims flow from its revanchist view of the past — a shifting standpoint that distorts history to help legitimise claims to territories long held by other countries. Changing the territorial status quo has been the unfinished business of the People's Republic of China since its founding in 1949, when it set out to forcibly absorb the sprawling Xinjiang and Tibetan plateau – actions that increased the landmass of China by 44 per cent. Underlining the fact that China does not apply the rule of law at home, its ingenious principle to covet neighbours' territories is: "what is ours is ours and what is yours is negotiable."[1] Maj Gen Zhang Zhaozhong (張召忠) of the People's Liberation Army (PLA) has interestingly termed this a "cabbage" strategy, which involves asserting a claim, launching furtive incursions into the coveted territory, and erecting – one at a time – cabbage-style multiple layers of security around a contested area so as deny access to a rival.[2] The establishment of an expansive air defence zone in the East China Sea is part of China's cabbage-style security layer move. By moving quietly and gradually to achieve a strategic transformation in its favour, China undercuts both the relevance of US security assurances to allies like Japan and the Philippines and the value of building countervailing strategic partnerships between and among Asian states and the United States. Taking on Japan, its former occupier and historical rival, is part of Beijing's larger search for new seabed resources and for strategic ascendancy in the western Pacific by breaking out of what it perceives to be the "first island chain" – a string of islands and atolls extending along China's eastern periphery that includes the Senkakus, Taiwan, and the

Paracel and Spratly Islands in the South China Sea. Its longer-term objective is to push US military assets to the "second island chain," farther out to the Pacific.[3]

Making an assessment of China's strategic thinking with regard to East Asian security, while the US-Japan alliance remains the cornerstone of Japanese diplomacy and foreign relations, appearing to stand firm, China's security perceptions of the region have undergone a sea of change. China's evolving equation with Russia, which itself is at loggerheads with the US and the West at large, is a testament to the great power game currently on display in Asia. Japan often suffers from what can be coined as the notion of the "alliance dilemma", with the United States being the only formal ally of Japan. Nations in an alliance relationship have two opposing kinds of fears – one is to be abandoned, while the other, is to be entangled in conflicts which the other partner gets involved in. During the early phase of the Cold War, Japan was entangled in the US-China confrontation. When President Nixon announced in July 1971 that he would visit China the following year, there was a sense that Japan was being abandoned, sidelined or surpassed. However, it turned to be a blessing in disguise and enabled Japan to establish diplomatic ties with China.[4] The credibility of American security assurances to its allies and partners shall remain the key. Future strategic equations in Asia will see the US being the key security provider, as well as states working in tandem to build power equilibrium.

Beijing's perspective of the Japan-US security alliance suggests it being influenced by China's normative views about the legitimacy of the security alliance. To a considerable extent, Chinese-Japanese political ties are a subset of China-US relations. In terms of Japan's role in this alliance, China observes that Japan seems to have made its strategic choice to ally with the 'existing declining power' to contain or hedge against the 'rising power' i.e. China. To the Chinese elites, this Japanese policy decision is short-sighted, unwise and unattainable in the long run.[5] The Chinese have been well aware that as an upright nationalist, Shinzo Abe was no less determined than Junichiro Koizumi to make Japan a "normal" state, to seek Japan's great power status and to contain China's growing influence in East Asia. What was interpreted by Japan as a wrong signal to Beijing in November 2011 was the US-China Joint Statement recorded between President Obama and President Hu when they agreed on "respecting each other's core interests as extremely important to ensure steady progress in US-China relations."[6] It is likely that this statement, among other key developments, has emboldened Beijing to take far more assertive actions in the South and East China Seas, defining them as an inherent part of its national "core interests." China officially began making declarations on what constitutes "core interests" in 2003, primarily to characterise Beijing's concern that Taiwan was steadily inching towards *de jure* independence. Even as Taiwan, Tibet, and Xinjiang have become salient to these claims, they have not remained limited to the same. Following the announcement of Taiwan being an area of core interest, Tibet and Xinjiang were subsequently declared the same in 2006. Since at least November of 2009, when it was inserted in the US-China Joint Statement between Hu Jintao and Barack Obama during the latter's state visit to China, the notion of China's "core interests" (核心利益) has received huge attention, among both media and experts alike. The use of this concept by the PRC government is an indication that the identified areas essentially remain non-negotiable in nature, thus, conveying a level of rigidity and perhaps militancy toward whatever issue might be defined as a core interest, including Taiwan, Tibet, Xinjiang and the South China Sea.[7] Given that the gambit of China's core interests critically includes state sovereignty, national security and reunification, the East China Sea resultantly shall also fall under this bracket.

On May 26, 2015, the Information Office of the State Council in Beijing released China's tenth defence-related White Paper, and the first-ever on "China's Military Strategy" *per se*. The White Paper outlines the possibility of both immediate and potential threats of local wars – for which, without "a strong military, a country can be neither safe nor strong." The main theme for the 2015 White Paper is the "long-standing task for China to safeguard its maritime rights and interests" – with special reference to the US' 'rebalancing' strategy and enhanced military presence and alliances in this region.[8] The White Paper mentions,

> Japan is sparing no effort to dodge the post-war mechanism, overhauling its military and security policies. Additionally, some of its offshore neighbors take provocative actions and reinforce their military presence on China's reefs and islands that they have illegally occupied. Some external countries are also busy meddling in South China Sea affairs; a tiny few maintain constant close-in air and sea surveillance and reconnaissance against China... The strategic task... to safeguard the security of China's overseas interests... The PLA Navy will gradually shift its focus from offshore waters defense to the combination of offshore waters defense with open seas protection...[9]

The Seemingly Unending Contest for Power and Influence

Contrary to the above discussed Chinese notions, the Japanese view is that managing growing Chinese power and influence and shaping China's strategic posture and policies would be critical for a new East Asian security order. There is a cultivated preference to believe, almost religiously, in the power of Article 9 of Japan's post-war Constitution as the guarantor of peace. The post-war politics of managing the alliance against the backdrop of an ideological tug of war over the post-war Constitution during the Cold War contributed to sustaining this idealistic—if not naïve—view of international politics. Japan faced acute challenges while rising from the ashes of defeat in World War II to become the world's second largest economy. This road of reconstruction to recovery became more challenging with the economic stagnation combined with the loss of strategic stability after the dissolution of the bipolar world order. The certainties of the Cold War era that allowed Japan to retain the political economy of "Japan, Inc." while being shielded by the US by virtue of the security alliance from the harsher realities of international security had crumbled.[10] This, in fact, represents one of the greatest challenges facing the Japanese leadership and the region at large, which fully comprehends that any movement on the Senkaku Islands issue shall most likely have a cascading impact on the Takeshima and Southern Kuril Islands issue that Japan is embroiled in with South Korea and Russia respectively.

Chinese scholars contend that Japan's international status has not declined, especially in East Asia where Japan continues to have considerable influence. Japan's economic standing, being the largest source of investment, and its strong presence in East Asia, will play a significant role in the future order of East Asia.[11] Moreover, as China's development will not cease, Japan's readjustment of its Asian and China policy will not be tactical, but strategic.[12] The accelerated integration of the regional economies with China and the fact that Beijing has become a central economic and political player not only in the region, but globally, presents profound strategic and possibly game-changing implications for a new 21st century international order.[13] Empirically and ideologically, the Senkaku/Diaoyu Islands dispute shall persist, neither reaching a peaceful settlement, nor escalating into a full-scale militarised conflict. Conventional explanations for this phenomenon have largely focussed on the following factors: the validity of contending historical evidence, domestic legitimisation processes, competition for energy and marine resources, historical animosities, and the role of the United States as an architect of the post-war Asian system. Despite their partial explanatory utility, these approaches cannot fully capture the continuing pattern of the rise and decline of conflict over the Senkaku/Diaoyu Islands.

To ensure that territorial disputes would cease to become a hotbed of contention, it can be concluded that careful drafting of the terms and conditions of the San Francisco Peace Treaty could have put an end to this quandary. Territorial provisions of the San Francisco Peace Treaty largely reflected the Allied powers' policy in East Asia, with the Allied powers more concerned with their own geo-political and strategic interests that resulted in a failure to resolve territorial disputes in East Asia.[14] Even if all the claimants (namely China, Japan and Taiwan) in the dispute over the Senkaku Islands, have international legal obligations in accordance with the UN Charter (under the principle of peaceful settlement of disputes), especially as articulated in Articles 2 and 33(1), the gaping institutional void on resolution of territorial disputes in the East Asian region, makes one sceptical about the likelihood of any resolution coming about any time soon.[15]

Chinese President Xi Jinping's promise of national greatness — embodied in the catchphrase "China dream" — is tied as much to achieving regional hegemony as to internal progress. The strategy bears all the hallmarks of modern Chinese brinkmanship, including reliance on stealth, surprise and a disregard for the risks of military escalation and seeks to ensure that the initiative remains with China. The pattern has become familiar: construct a dispute, initiate a jurisdictional claim through periodic incursions, and then increase the frequency and duration of such intrusions, thereby establishing a military presence or pressuring a rival to cut a deal on China's terms. This shrewdness not only keeps opponents off balance, but also undercuts the relevance of US security assurances to allies and the value of building countervailing strategic partnerships in Asia. In fact, by camouflaging offence as defence, China casts the burden of starting a war on an opponent, while it seeks to lay the foundation — brick by brick — of a hegemonic Middle Kingdom – seeking to achieve a position strong enough to get its way without having to fire a shot.[16] Discussing China's "disputes in territorial waters" (领土领海争端) Chu Shulong points out that China has only recently started to concern itself with maritime issues, coming to a new realisation that it is not only a "continental Loess civilisation" (黄土文明 *huangtu wenming*) but also a "marine blue civilisation" (蔚蓝色文明 *weilanse wenming*).[17]

China argues that the Diaoyu Islands reverted to China in pursuance to the 1951 San Francisco Peace

Treaty and the 1952 Sino-Japanese Peace Treaty. Contrarily, Japan claims that under Article III of the San Francisco Peace Treaty, the islands were included as part of the Ryukyu Islands and placed under US administrative control, only to be returned to Japan as per the US' Okinawa Reversion Agreement with Tokyo in 1971. The question of ascertaining *terra nullius* status remains the core issue in this dispute, because the *terra nullius* status is directly related to the question of whether the Treaty of Shimonoseki, indeed, included the disputed islands or not. Hypothetically, if the islands indeed were *terra nullius* in 1895, would it be necessary for them to be included in the Treaty of Shimonoseki? The answer would be NO, because it defies logic for one to cede territory that one does not own, or exercise sovereignty.[18] Japan, without doubt, has a relatively stronger, superior and valid claim to title over the Senkaku Islands based on effective occupation and continuous display of state function and administration over the islands ever since January 14, 1895. Japan has been controlling the Senkaku Island chain since 1895. Under Article Three of the San Francisco Treaty of 1951 when the Senkaku Island chain came under US administration, no objection was raised by Beijing. In 1969, when the Okinawa Diversion Treaty was signed under which the US pledged to return Okinawa and the islands southwest of Okinawa, including Senkaku, there was no objection from China. In 1972, when Okinawa and the southwestern islands were returned to Japan, there was no objection. Only in the second half of the 1970s, when the issue of developing petroleum resources on the continental shelf of the East China Sea came up, did China suddenly express interest in the Senkaku Islands issue.

Defining Sovereign Boundaries and its Legality

Reaching a broad consensus on how nations can acquire territory and preserve their own sovereign boundaries – forming a clear definition of what it means to be an administrating state, rather than a pure sovereign state – should be a priority. The lack of international legal guiding principles on the difference between administrative powers and sovereign powers fosters greater confusion on the issue and encourages a few countries to implicitly suggest that there is no distinction at all.[19] However, given what is at stake, the concern that nations promoting their own political agendas cannot be the sole motivation to avoid work on a convention to elucidate territorial disputes, as per this argument, would excuse inaction on any number of important international legal issues.[20] Contemporary international law contains a relevant toolbox for peaceful settlement of international disputes, as outlined in Article 33 of the UN Charter. Direct negotiation between the parties concerned appears to be the most pertinent avenue for resolving a territorial dispute. The UN Charter states that parties to any dispute, the continuance of which is likely to endanger the maintenance of international peace and security, shall, first of all, seek a solution by negotiation, enquiry, mediation, conciliation, arbitration, judicial settlement, resort to regional agencies or arrangements, or other peaceful means of their own choice [UN Charter, Article 33(4)]. Settling territorial disputes by judicial decision or arbitration merely confirms the existence of title, and judgements by the international court or arbitral tribunal are, in a "majority of cases, declaratory rather than constitutive." Boundary or arbitral awards are, therefore, not the foundation of title to territory. Regarding the International Court of Justice (ICJ) at The Hague, once the parties submit their case to the ICJ, Article 60 states, "The Court's judgment is final and without appeal." More importantly, should one of the states involved fail to comply with the court's decision, the other party may have recourse to the United Nations Security Council.[21] Japan has the edge when it comes to putting forth its claim over the Senkaku Islands, because, as the Chamber of the ICJ has repeatedly demonstrated over the years, the exercise of sovereign authority over island territories is the key factor in determining ownership of islands. Therein lies the strength of Japan's claim, that of exercising sovereignty continuously since 1895.[22]

In the event of Japan and China submitting their respective case/position over the Diaoyu/Senkaku Islands to the ICJ, the adjudicating Chamber of the ICJ would primarily look into the archival historical records of the exercise of authority by each sovereign over the islands. For all these queries to be addressed, research and analysis need to be conducted with complete access to all relevant materials and historical records, which currently are not entirely placed in the declassified public domain. Though inequitable in a historical context, under the current law governing territorial disputes over islands, the ICJ would likely find that Japan's post-war peaceful exercise of actual authority over the islands shall quash China's so-called "historical claim".[23] The issue of private ownership of the islands is not relevant to resolving the sovereignty question. Private or public property rights over the islands do not affect the sovereignty status of the islands under international law. However, simultaneously, the presence of fishermen in the surrounding areas of the disputed islands too, does not constitute a solid legal foundation for a nation to lay claim over sovereignty. For instance, in the Case Concerning Sovereignty over Pulau Ligitan and Pulau Sipadan (Indonesia vs. Malaysia), Indonesia argued that the traditional use of waters surrounding certain disputed islands by Indonesian fishermen supported its claim to sovereignty [Sovereignty over Pulau Ligitan and Pulau Sipadan (Indon. /Malay.) 2002 I.C.J. 625, *para* 140 (December 17)]. However, the International Court of Justice rejected that argument and explained that the "activities by private persons cannot be seen as [evidence of sovereignty] if they do not take place on the basis of official regulations or under governmental authority." In fact, the basic contours of this rule have been in place since at least the 19th century.[24]

There is no competent international court or tribunal to address the issue of sovereignty over these islands. The International Court of Justice, or any other tribunal, can come into play only when the parties to the dispute have in some way given their consent. Even if the sovereignty issue has been resolved, the parties will still have to agree on an "equitable" delimitation of their EEZ boundaries. Bilateral discussions during working-level talks held in Beijing way back in November 1980 revealed that there existed too large a gap between the two governments' opinions on how to properly delimit the continental shelf. The conflicting opinions were as follows: "If the area covered by joint development extended right up to the Okinawa trough, the Japanese would have felt that the Chinese would gain a lot without giving away anything. Whereas for the Chinese government, if joint development was limited to the continental shelf on the Chinese side of the median line between the baselines of the two countries, it would be... the only party making a concession."[25] Therefore, should they not be able to reach an agreement, or even a mutual settlement for that matter, the dispute can only be settled thereafter by a court or tribunal if the parties have given their consent.[26] It remains highly unlikely, to the extent of being impossible, that China and Japan will resort to take the matter to the ICJ, in that both would not want to risk an adverse decision.

Senkaku Islands : An Interminable Strategic Contest

Opinions on China's strategy range widely from objectives and principles to the values that China's foreign policy appears to be pursuing and is driven by. The perspectives range from being extreme nationalist to being liberal internationalist. The decline of political ideology has been compensated for by the embrace of nationalism – in fact, that of ultra-nationalism. Nationalism has become a vehicle for fashioning a state's political resurgence, argues Brahma Chellaney.[27] China does not hide its ambition to be the dominant player. In fact, it wants a unipolar Asia while it tries for a multipolar world. Nationalism is the undercurrent driving the attitudes and aspirations of nations, especially Japan and China, towards each other. Chinese scholar Shi Yinhong points out that the contemporary nationalism in China is not only a decisive force in driving forward the process of reform essential to China's modernisation but also an important conduit for preserving China's traditional features. According to Shi, Chinese nationalism is mainly characterised by foresightedness, calmness, patience and respect for tradition.[28] What Shi fails to identify or discuss further, is where individual aspiration, liberties, and freedom to exercise choices lie in China. Another Chinese scholar, Zi Zhongyun, argues that China's development over the past few decades has taken place in the context of a struggle between tradition and reform. Nationalism (patriotism) and internationalism represent the opposite poles of this struggle. Having been accumulated over many years, Chinese nationalism has prevailed over reforms driving towards modernisation'.[29]

Shinzo Abe has averred that the relationship with China is one of the most important bilateral relationships for Japan, and has accepted the need for a dialogue – however, without attaching any preconditions. Circuitously, Abe was referring to the Chinese demand/precondition of any Japanese Prime Minister not visiting the Yakusuni War Shrine again. Besides, China's and Japan's deep economic interdependence means that both sides have compelling incentives to manage their relationship carefully; indeed, both countries have displayed a high degree of pragmatism in avoiding being influenced by their respective nationalistic constituencies in actual crises and, at the same time, averting any encroachment on their sovereignty claims. Even if the initial problem concerning the delimitation of the continental shelf can be overcome, considering the historical animosity and mutual suspicion that has characterised past Sino-Japanese relations, one cannot refrain from wondering whether further issues of management and apportionment of the islands' resources and subsequent economic returns can be easily agreed upon.[30] Zhu Feng proposes a three-pronged strategy to "protect the islands" centred on three principles: (1) complete military preparedness (充分的军事准备 *chongfen de junshi zhunbei*); (2) effective crisis diplomacy (成

功的危机外交 *chenggong de weiji waijiao*); and (3) combining the efforts of the Chinese government and society (中国政府与社会共同努 *Zhongguo zhengfu yu shehui gongtong nuli*). Zhu terms the Japanese right wing as "a common enemy of the political community of East Asia" (东亚政治共同的敌人, *dongya zhengzhi gongtong de diren*). In an international crisis like the dispute over the Diaoyu Islands, "effective crisis diplomacy" must be implemented as soon as possible to reassert China's position. Zhao Quansheng and Wu Di propose an economic solution to the stand-off. Zhao says China should use its economic dominance to put pressure on Japan, since Japan's economy is suffering from a "terminal illness of the economy" (经济绝症 *jingji juezheng*).[31]

Subsequent Japanese administrations have found it challenging to bluntly curb nationalist groups' activities, both because they share nationalist persuasions, and because they cannot take strong measures – which is an obvious asymmetry between the two countries. Focussing on China's policy, three trends in particular, are noteworthy: (1) China's increasing willingness and ability to deploy military forces in the East China Sea; (2) China's growing capacity to exploit the resources in, or close to, the disputed area; (3) the increasingly prominent role of anti-Japanese grassroots organisations within China.[32] The last facet is especially important because it signifies that popular nationalism cannot be understood within a 'state-over society' view of Chinese politics. The Party-state is clearly losing its control over the innumerable cyber-nationalist manifestations – indicators that often seemingly merge into criticism of the Chinese government for being soft on Japan. The authorities clearly intend to impose the government's will and policy on the netizens, but public opinion on the net cannot be effectively silenced despite the persistence of state censorship.[33] While the temptation to beat the anti-Japanese nationalist drum has become harder to resist, it has also become more dangerous as the Party-state may lose control when it feels that it has to respond to increasingly popular and strident anti-Japanese groups.[34] The central point is that the fundamental goals of China as a country of strongly growing prosperity and the 'reform and opening project' may be lost if the Party-state cannot control nationalist demands for more unilateral actions.

The Yoshihiko Noda government felt compelled to act preemptively for fear that if Ishihara purchased the islands and built structures on them, a far larger crisis would result and send tensions with China spiralling. Recall that Shintaro Ishihara, the then Governor of Tokyo, had announced on April 16, 2012, a plan for the Tokyo metropolitan government to purchase three of the Diaoyu/Senkaku Islands from the Kurihara family and build on them, citing the need to counter China's challenge to Japanese control.[35] Subsequently, the Noda government was apprehensive that it lacked the legal means to stop Ishihara, and due to the significant public support for the Tokyo Governor's plan to purchase the islands, it decided in May 2012 to open its own bid to purchase them.[36] Noda was also reportedly driven by "a sense of responsibility" to defend the country's territory.[37] Accordingly, Noda announced in September 2012 that Japan would purchase or "re-nationalise" the three islets formerly owned by the government, and prior to this announcement, sent his special envoy to Beijing to explain that the purchase was aimed at the peaceful and stable maintenance and management of the islands. Prime Minister Noda also met President Hu Jintao in Vladivostok just before the purchase to explain his intentions, but Hu did not accept Noda's move toward nationalisation. Beijing considered the purchase a deliberate unilateral change to the status quo. Many Chinese analysts adopted the narrative of a "good cop, bad cop" conspiracy by Japan to solidify its claim. Policy groupthink – where lower-level analysts and bureaucrats assess the leadership's position and provide information and analysis accordingly – reinforced their belief that Noda had engineered the drama with Ishihara to deal a blow to China. The Chinese policy apparatus, given the very different political and legal systems in the two countries, easily adopted this version. In contrast with Japan, Chinese regional officials who oversee provinces are appointed and rotated by the central government, and "respond to signals set by the centralised Party leadership".[38]

Tokyo had most naturally expected a negative reaction from China, but was trying not to "lose bigger" should Ishihara purchase and develop the islands. Not surprisingly, the Chinese authorities openly encouraged the protesters to vent their anger on the sovereignty issue – a rare and next to impossible sight in China, where popular rallies are considered forbidden and unimaginable. However, this has a perilous flipside to it. The central point is that, given the lack of democratic and parliamentary mechanisms for influencing the decision-makers, the Internet is a useful outlet for nationalist groups to let off steam, notwithstanding that the authorities are often successful in attempts to restrain their communications.[39] A specific feature of the domestic situation is that the PLA's preference for firmness and strong anti-Japanese attitudes could play together with popular nationalism, ending up squeezing the civilian leaders into a confrontation with Japan, even though the PLA's loyalty to the Party-state is beyond doubt.[40] The critical problem lies in the socio-economic sphere in China. If a new crisis were to take place in a situation of major failure and collapse of the Chinese economy, especially if the failure is caused by corruption and economic mismanagement by the CCP's leadership, it would clearly be more difficult to stifle public protests before they become a threat to the Party-state, especially if nationalist movements fuse various discontented groups under the banner of nationalism.[41] Moreover, in the event of factions within the CCP using nationalism to challenge and attack (persons holding positions in) the current leadership for not defending China's core interests with sufficient vigour, a real threat may develop, and the Party-state's efforts to maintain legitimacy by stirring up nationalism may backfire.[42]

The study of popular nationalism in China's East China Sea policy stands incomplete without an observation on the role of history in Asian and Western foreign policies. Kishore Mahbubani, an incisive observer of contrasts between Asian and Western diplomatic styles, notes that China's leaders can "switch off" the past. Even though China's pragmatic leaders have displayed an impressive ability to implement Janus-like policies, they have not been able wholly to switch off the past in the way Mao and his diplomatic master, Chou Enlai, could. Otherwise expressed, the totalitarian Chinese system under Mao could switch off the past more easily than today's leaders of a more democratic, but still authoritarian, political system. Here Max Weber's famous observation: "It is not true that good can follow only good and evil only evil" – is pertinent.[43] Thus, prospects of presenting the islands dispute to the ICJ coupled with the following political circumstances confronting the disputants need to be pointed out. Foremost is the issue concerning the status of the Republic of China (Taiwan) in the international community.

Bringing the islands dispute before the ICJ is an option concerning only the PRC and Japan, since both nations are current members of the UN and signatories to the Statute of the ICJ.[44] Unless the political contest between the PRC and ROC ceases to exist, it would be naïve to envisage any trilateral agreements for the development of the potential hydrocarbon resources in the seabed appertaining to the disputed islands. In this reference, it is vital to mention former Taiwanese President Ma Ying-jeou's August 2012 proposal initiative calling for peace titled the East China Sea Peace Initiative (ECSPI) which specifically catered to the Senkaku/Islands.[45] The ECSPI places emphasis on establishing a code of conduct for the East China Sea, developing programmes for joint conservation, management and extraction of natural resources, and some form of joint exercises to maintain peace and stability in the disputed territories. The initiative is based on the concept that while sovereignty is indivisible, resources can be shared, thereby suggesting facilitation of a dialogue, shelving territorial disputes through negotiations, formulating a Code of Conduct in the East China Sea and engaging in joint development of resources. President Ma Ying-jeou emphasised on the importance of air space security in the East China Sea during an international conference on "Peace and Security in East Asia", comprising three major points: (1) all parties concerned should abide by the principles of international law and in the spirit of the East China Sea Peace Initiative, ensure air space safety to safeguard freedom of aviation; (2) parties with overlapping air defence identification zones should seek provisional arrangements so as to avoid miscalculation, and reduce the impact on freedom and safety of aviation; (3) the parties should jointly negotiate the formulation of an "East China Sea Code of Conduct" concerning both maritime space and air space.[46]

Negotiating a solution could include an agreement on provisional arrangements of a practical nature; for instance, no action may be undertaken which would aggravate the dispute. There is a need to explore the natural resources cooperatively for which arrangements are already in place in many areas of the world, including joint development schemes between Malaysia and Thailand, and between Vietnam and Thailand in the Gulf of Thailand that provide for the joint exploitation of natural resources in the area of overlapping claims. Reference may also be made to the agreement (but which does not provide for actual joint development) reached by China and Japan in 2008 to develop cooperatively the undersea Chunxiao/Shirakaba oil and gas field, an area located to the north of the Diaoyu/Senkaku Islands. In this agreement (called "Principled Consensus" in China), the two states agreed, in order to make the East China Sea a "Sea of Peace, Cooperation and Friendship", to cooperate, without prejudice, to their legal positions, during the transitional period pending agreement on the delimitation. Such arrangements could also be a first step for dealing with the other disputed parts of the East China Sea. However, it should be noted that the 2008 Agreement does not involve an area where a dispute over island territory is involved. Similarly, there could be prospects of setting up a cooperative development zone for joint development of the natural resources surrounding the islands. Another alternative is to establish a joint development zone for the exploration of natural resources around the region surrounding the islands in a cooperative effort while leaving aside the issue of sovereignty. This offers an interim solution in which neither state renounces its sovereignty claim to the islands nor recognises the legitimacy of another state's claim while making it possible to address resource problems.[47]

In furtherance to this proposal, the Special Political and Decolonialisation Committee, with sponsor Australia *recommends* the creation of the Pacific Group, to meet annually to discuss matters relating to trade, stability and further integration in the region of the Pacific, the Philippine and China Seas, and to include the following members: Australia, Republic of China, People's Republic of China, Indonesia, Japan, Republic of Korea, Papua New Guinea, the Philippines, the United States of America and Vietnam, and be sponsored by Japan. It *further recommends* that 70 per cent of all revenue of potential oil reserves in the territorial waters of the Senkaku/Diaoyu Islands, if exploited, be put into a fund administered by the members of the Pacific Group with the objective of promoting regional stability, cooperation and understanding, and the remaining 30 per cent be allocated to the People's Republic of China.[48]Akikazu Hashimoto, Michael O'Hanlon and Wu Xinbo offered a multi-pronged plan under which China and Japan could well promise not to raise new territorial disputes in the future with the parties agreeing to decouple EEZ determinations from sovereignty over the islands themselves. Further, each side would acknowledge the other's territorial claims and Japan would delegate rights of administration to a joint oversight board, with authority to regulate patrols and usage. The authors view their approach as "designed to respect the core interests and non-negotiable demands of both claimants to the islands."

Realistically speaking, all these proposals seem far-fetched and implausible given that the Japanese Prime Minister, while addressing the UN General Assembly, on September 26, 2012, stated emphatically, "... as far as the Senkaku Islands are concerned, they are an inherent part of our territory in the light of history and also in international law. There are no territorial issues as such. Therefore, there can be no compromise." Chinese Foreign Minister Yang Jiechi responded to the General Assembly the next day: "The moves taken by Japan are totally illegal and invalid. They can in no way change the historical fact that Japan stole Diaoyu and its affiliated islands from China and the fact that China has territorial sovereignty over them." Zhongqi Pan, an Associate Professor at the School of International Relations and Public Affairs at China's Fudan University, argues that maintaining status quo perhaps is the most likely prospect of the dispute in the foreseeable future.[49] As long as the pending dispute does not pop up to the top of the agenda in Sino-Japanese relations, both China and Japan can be expected to not make solving the dispute their first priority. Due to the complicated and difficult nature of contemporary Sino-Japanese relations, a breakthrough in the dispute over the Senkaku Islands seems very unlikely. The "new thinking" regarding Sino-Japanese relations, according to Ye Zicheng, may be summed up as: (1) find a common denominator of bilateral political and economic interests and seek a breakthrough in bilateral relations; (2) pursue common interests within a multilateral framework and promote establishment of a new political and economic order in East Asia; and (3) establish a system in which China and Japan play equally important roles based on cooperation, instead of competition, for leadership in East Asia.[50] However, despite the two governments' efforts to launch various dialogue mechanisms, including the China-Japan Strategic Dialogue, High-Level Economic Dialogue, consultation on issues related to the East China Sea, and defence and security consultation, there is no crisis management mechanism between China and Japan. This is why, should either/both sides attempt to employ force to change the status quo, it would have an extremely deleterious effect on Sino-Japanese relations, and on East Asian security at large. As a first step toward demonstrating a genuine intention to preserve peace, escalatory actions and aggressive rhetoric need to cease. Given that peaceful resolution of the sovereignty dispute is not immediately attainable, managing the dispute remains the most viable option. The shared desire to avoid a military conflict and complementary economic ties offer substantive incentive and common ground for the two most prominent East Asian nations to engage eloquently.

The core assumption of liberal theories that interdependence among states influences state behaviour, much in divergence to realists,[51] cannot be confirmed as being germane to the Japan-China case where the acrimonious history and resurgent nationalism in both states has impacted directly on the security equation between the two – as my book argues. Underpinning scepticism of China's peaceful rise is a compelling formulation of the offensive realism by theorists like John Mearsheimer, whose version of offensive realism theory is diverse from Kenneth Waltz's defensive realist theory. Mearsheimer concludes that states will *ceaselessly pursue power* while Waltz emphasises how the balance-of-power constrains power-maximising behaviour and makes states content *once they have enough power to be secure.*[52] The Chinese case could be argued as one of application of offensive realism, which interprets power as *shi* (勢) – held as the ultimate source of security and manifested in the form of pursuing regional hegemony. The demonstrations against Japan have been perpetrated as the most potent form of 'popular nationalism', closely hitched to China's pursuit of its territorial goals. Nationalism and territory have always been intertwined and can create incentives for expansion. China emphasises not just on physical means but also non-physical means in military affairs and warfare, and has incorporated the concept of *Three Warfares,* namely, *Media Warfare*, *Psychological Warfare*, and *Legal Warfare,* into the tasks of the political work of the military. *Media Warfare* is aimed at influencing domestic and international public opinion to build public and international support for China's military actions and to dissuade an adversary from pursuing policies perceived to be adverse to China's interests. *Psychological Warfare* seeks to undermine the adversary's ability to conduct combat operations through psychological operations aimed at deterring, shocking, and demoralising enemy military personnel and supporting civilian populations. And *Legal Warfare* uses international and domestic laws to gain international support and manage possible political repercussions of China's military actions.[53]

The preference among militaries for offensive doctrines offers a potential logic of expansion – often referred to as the "cult of the offensive". The Chinese military's core doctrinal principle still is Mao Zedong's concept of "active defence" (*jiji fangyu*), sometimes described also as "offensive defence" (*gongshifangyu*)[54] which appears entirely appropriate in this case. The rise of China is likely, or nearly inevitably, to cause regional instability, volatility and conflict much in resemblance to the time gone by when Athenian historian, political philosopher and General, Thucydides deemed the Peloponnesian War predestined as he recounted the 5th century BC war between Sparta and Athens to the year 411 BC, when Athens rose, and the relative power of Sparta declined.[55]

The view in a few quarters in Washington hinges upon concerns about Shinzo Abe potentially viewing US treaty guarantees as a shield for Japan to confront an increasingly assertive China in the East China Sea – further crystallising the dilemma between a revisionist China and a militarily resurgent Japan. The deep, yet complex interweaving of the Sino-US relationship gets reflected with China as the biggest buyer of the US Treasury, however, at the same time, with Washington's inherent discomfort with the potential reality of the emergence of a Sino-centric Asia. Although the Senkaku Islands do not define the overall relationship between China and Japan, in the larger geo-strategic campaign in East Asia, it most certainly has become a perfect alibi/policy tool for defence and foreign policy announcements.

Most certainly, China can ill-afford losing credibility at home (more specifically, in the context of Japan, over the Senkaku Islands issue), which could become the driver for China's leadership to respond decisively with greater aggressiveness rather than withdrawal in regional disputes. China characterises the initial two decades of the 21st century as a "period of strategic opportunity", and the phenomenal rise and strengthening of China's *comprehensive national power*, will be instrumental to perpetuate the rule of the Party, ensure lasting domestic stability, sustain and defend national sovereignty and territorial integrity and, ultimately, secure and seal China's status as a resurgent great power. These objectives have often been rolled into Xi Jinping's "China dream". What is most critical in here is the timing, with 2021 establishing 100 years since the founding of the Chinese Communist Party and 2049 ushering in 100 years of the People's Republic of China coming into existence as a nation-state. Realisation of these twin bicentennial goals remains the nucleus of Xi Jinping's "China dream" – most significantly including the vital goal of national rejuvenation (read reunification) encapsulating a long-standing national aspiration of establishing a powerful and prosperous China. Notwithstanding that Xi's political standing and control at present pronounce him as China's most powerful ruler since Deng Xiaoping, and possibly even since Mao, it simultaneously brings to light the nation's tempestuous political past when Chairman Mao's reign was notoriously reminiscent of the turbulences of a brutal dictatorship. It needs to be recalled that over-centralisation of power by Mao and Deng, came at the expense of their elite. Although Xi Jinping is attempting to add a rather awkward dash of populism to his rule, the concurrent tightening of control on online social networks and brute crackdown against political dissent/activism shall blemish the idea of Xi's "China dream"—a dream that is already marred by serious discontinuities stretching from a slowing growth trajectory, growing debt projection, continuing political instability in restive regions and a larger economic slowdown, all of which, Xi will be forced to effectively grapple with.

The 501-page verdict delivered on July 12, 2016, by the Permanent Court of Arbitration (PCA) at The Hague, on the complaint filed by the Philippines vis-à-vis the South China Sea issue has favoured the Philippines and given a judgement which is unambiguous and categorical on sovereignty claims, environmental issues, fisheries, and freedom of navigation. The decision announced by the PCA goes considerably beyond the issues raised by the Philippines and effectively demolishes the arguments advanced by China. The Permanent Court of Arbitration has dismissed China's very basic contention that its claims date back to the 2nd century BC and ruled that China has no legal basis for its maritime territorial claims over 3.5 million sq km (nearly 90 per cent) of the South China Sea, nor over its undersea mineral and other resources. More so, the so-called 'nine-dash' line used by Beijing since May 2009 when it submitted a map detailing this line to the United Nations, to delineate its South China Sea claims is in contravention to the United Nations convention on maritime law. The July 12 decision is a definite setback to China's assiduous efforts since at least 1974 to build a case for its claims of sovereignty over the South China Sea. The verdict is direct, and unusual, in so far as countering China's niftily crafted discourse of "historical and indisputable" claims over of over 90 per cent of the South China Sea.[56] The court slammed China for obstructing the Filipino fishermen's livelihood, and clarified that sovereignty claims cannot be obtained through historical claims or artificial reef build-up, and that, international trade should not be impeded by any country.

China has suffered immense loss of face internationally due to the verdict of the International Court of Justice, which is expected to have a long-term impact on China's domestic politics as well. The verdict will be gradually played out in the Communist Party's factional struggles and could well be a portent for gradual change in China's politics, although Leninist 'centralism' might likely come to the rescue of the powers-that-be in the near term.[57] However, despite the PCA's verdict against China on the militarisation of the region, Beijing is unlikely to vacate the artificial reefs or remove missile batteries and other military assets from the region – and this defiance will deal a crushing blow to international law. China could now double down on its defiance, by establishing an ADIZ in the South China Sea – a move that would effectively prohibit flights through the region without Chinese permission. Given that China has already militarised the area, including building radar facilities on new islets, construction of airfields, communications facilities and gun emplacements, and deploying the 100-kilometre-range HQ-9 surface-to-air missiles on Woody Island, it is well positioned to enforce such an ADIZ.[58] In an expected move, China's President and Chairman of the Central Military Commission, Xi Jinping placed the People's Liberation Army on 'secondary alert' to 'check all the possibilities' and 'prepare to make war.' The PLA's Southern Theatre Command, the PLA Navy's South China Sea Fleet, Air Force and Rocket Forces have reportedly been placed on 'pre-war status.' The decision has isolated China internationally and has strengthened the principled positions of nations, including Japan, against which Beijing is working relentlessly to challenge the territorial status quo in the East China Sea over the Senkaku Islands. Unsurprisingly, Japan has come out in full support of the PCA's verdict against China.

The strategic location of the East China Sea is vital to comprehend the power play on display. It is a semi-closed sea bordered by the Yellow Sea to the north, the South China Sea and Taiwan to the south, Japan's Ryukyu and Kyushu Islands to the east and the Chinese mainland to the west. The area around Senkaku is placed in close proximity to important shipping lanes, offering rich fishing grounds and holding a rich seabed of potential oil and gas reserves underneath. As the strategic competition between regional and global players over gaining primacy in the Asia Pacific increases, the Senkaku Island dispute is only expected to heighten in the coming future, thereby challenging the already fragile balance of power in East Asia. China's meteoric rise in economic heft, military muscle, and political clout over the past three decades has not only dramatically revamped the world's most populous nation, it has also decisively shaped East Asia's post-Cold War geo-political landscape. The lack of transparency and ambiguity about how China intends to use its newfound power—to reinforce existing international norms, to revise them according to Beijing's national interests, or both — continues to endure as an area of growing concern. The Senkaku Islands is an issue, which the Chinese government will just not give up – more so, now, with Beijing having the will and confidence to pursue this challenge.

In this reference, there appears a close linkage between the *Peripheral Diplomacy Initiative* announced in October 2013 during the Chinese Communist Party's unprecedented work forum (*zuotan* 座谈) on Chinese diplomacy toward the periphery (*zhoubian* 周边) i.e., the land and maritime areas adjacent to China. What needs to be underlined here is that the ADIZ was established and announced by China exactly one month after the announcement of the Peripheral Diplomacy Initiative. Similarly, the new Xi doctrine of building a Chinese "maritime great wall" represents a red line, which should not be crossed. The contemporary thought in China is "... you push me and I will push you back, because I have the capability to do it now..." Now that China has acquired the military muscle following a protracted stint of its military's modernisation, it is employing that muscle, albeit in a strategically astute manner. Japan, territorially, is a status quo power vis-à-vis China, and Beijing is surreptitiously upping the ante against Japan in the East China Sea to test the tenacity of the US-Japan alliance. With a Chinese frigate (3,900-ton Jiangkai class) sailing for the first time through the "contiguous zone" near the Senkaku Islands on June 09, 2016, the writing on the wall is apparently quite clear – Beijing is attempting to burnish a no-compromise stance on territorial issues in both the East China Sea and South China Sea. The *Nikkei Asian Review* reported that the PLAN vessel did not enter Japan's territorial waters, since it would have been an act that would constitute a violation of international law. Instead, the frigate sailed through a so-called contiguous zone (an area of water that extends as far as 24 nautical miles out from territorial seas) probably to avoid a direct confrontation with Japan and the US. Moreover, China has installed radar equipment on a gas exploration platform close to disputed waters in the East China Sea. The concern surrounding this radar emanates primarily in that, this radar, a type commonly found on patrol ships and not necessary for gas field development, could be a sign that China intends to use gas exploration platforms in the disputed waters as military stations. Consequently, Japan lodged an official protest on August 5, 2016 through its embassy in China, urging Beijing to explain the purpose.

The dependence of Japan on the US for ensuring the security cover suits China at this point in time, rather than Tokyo asserting its military prowess more independently. This, however, shall challenge the maritime aspirations of the PLA Navy in the larger Asia-Pacific, given the advanced naval capabilities and/or force protection capability of the US in terms of the range of its military bases and the number of its allies and partners. China's status and growing assertive role and presence in the East Asian region pave the way for continuing American engagement and forging countervailing geo-strategic partnerships with the Asian states that share common objectives. That said, China will continue to press its claims to Taiwan, in the East and South China Seas, and over disputed territory with India, and it will use diplomatic, paramilitary and coercive military tactics to do so. China will continue to use external tensions and the tool of fervent nationalism to mobilise domestic political support and will attempt to use its growing military and paramilitary capabilities for coercive purposes – in a desperate effort to revise the regional order in Asia, step by step, only underlining its revisionist aspirations and geo-strategic conduct.

Notes

1. Brahma Chellaney, "For China, Border Row with India a means to Keep it under Pressure," *Hindustan Times*, June 13, 2015.
2. Brahma Chellaney, "Irredentist China Ups the Ante," *Forbes*, December 01, 2013.
3. Ibid.
4. Views of Professor Seiichiro Takagi, available at https://www.wilsoncenter.org/sites/default/files/Hill%20Event%20Transcript%20-Final.pdf
5. Wang Jian Wei, "The US-Japan Alliance in the 21st Century: A Chinese Perspective" in Purnendra Jain and Lam Peng Er, eds., *Japan's Strategic Challenges in a Changing Regional Environment* (MA: World Scientific Publishing Co. Pte. Ltd., 2013), pp. 25-27.
6. For more details, see "US-China Joint Statement," Office of the Press Secretary, The White House, November 17, 2009.

7. Michael D. Swaine, "China's Assertive Behavior-Part One: On 'Core Interests'," *China Leadership Monitor*, No. 34, Winter 2011.
8. Dennis J. Blasko, "The 2015 Chinese Defense White Paper on Strategy in Perspective: Maritime Missions Require a Change in the PLA Mindset," *China Brief,* Jamestown Foundation, Vol. 15, No. 2, May 29, 2015.
9. For more details, see White Paper on *China's Military Strategy*, released by the State Council, Information Office of the People's Republic of China, Beijing, May 2015.
10. Satoh Haruko, "Rethinking Security in Japan: In Search of a Post-'Postwar' Narrative" in Jain and Er, n. 5, pp. 288-293.
11. Song Guoyou, "Shixi Riben de Dongya Diqu Zhixu Zhanlue", *Guoji Luntan,* No. 5, 2007, p. 64, cited in Zhu Liqun, "China's Foreign Policy Debates," *Chaillot Papers* (121), Institute for Security Studies, European Union, Paris, September 2010.
12. Sun Cheng, "*Cong 'JianzhiguanWaijiao' 'Dao Jiji de Yazhou Waijiao' – 'Riben Anbei, Futian Neige Yazhou Waijiao de Bijiao Fenxi,*" *Guoji Wenti Yanjiu*, No. 2, 2008, pp. 42-46.
13. Katahara Eiichi, "Japan's Strategic Options?" in Jain and Er, n. 5, p. 7.
14. For more details on this subject, see Chi Manjiao, "The Unhelpfulness of Treaty Law in Solving the Sino-Japan Sovereign Dispute over the Diaoyu Islands", Paper presented at the International Symposium on Dokdo Islands: Sovereignty Dispute in East Asia, Washington D.C., May 20, 2010, cited in the *University of Pennsylvania East Asia Law Review.*
15. For more details, see UN Charter Art. 2, 33, *para.* 1; also see, MK Young, "Regional Institutions in East Asia and the Pacific: Is the Time Ripe?"*PROCEEDINGS* 471, 1995; and see, G. Triggs, "Confucius and Consensus: International Law in the Asian Pacific," *Melbourne University Law Review*, No. 650, 1997.
16. Brahma Chellaney, "China's Creeping 'Cabbage' Strategy", *Taipei Times*, December 01, 2013.
17. Chu Shulong, "The Current Situation in Remote Chinese Territorial Waters and its External Strategic Design", *Xiandai Guoji Guanxi,*

Journal of the China Institute of Contemporary International Relations, No. 8, 2012; for more details, see the Report by the Asia Centre, European Council on Foreign Relations, "Shockwaves from the China/Japan Island Dispute," February 2013.

18. Caleb Wan, "Security Flashpoint: International Law and the Islands Dispute in the Far East," *New Zealand Post-Graduate Law e-Journal*, No. 2, 2005.
19. R Jade Harry, "A Solution Acceptable to All? A Legal Analysis of the Senkaku-Diaoyu Island Dispute," *Cornell International Law Journal*, Vol. 46, No. 653, 2013, p. 233.
20. Ibid.
21. n. 15, Art. 94(2).
22. William B Heflin, "Diaoyu/Senkaku Islands Dispute: Japan and China, Oceans Apart," *Asian-Pacific Law & Policy Journal*, Vol. 18, No. 1, 2000, Hawaii, p. 123.
23. Ibid., pp. 125-128.
24. For more details, see Sir Robert Phillimore, *Commentaries upon International Law* (London: Butterworths, 1879).
25. Chi-kin Lo, *China's Policy towards Territorial Disputes: The Case of the South China Sea Islands* (Routledge: London, 1989), p. 174.
26. Alfred Soons and Nico Schrijver, "What Does International Law say About the China-Japan Dispute over the Diaoyu/Senkaku Islands?" *Briefing Paper*, The Hague Institute for Global Justice, December 03, 2012.
27. Brahma Chellaney's views during the course of a conversation with the author.
28. Shi Yinhong, "*Zhongguo Lishi Zhizhong de Lianxu he Biange yu Zhongguo Xiandangdai Minzu Zhuyi*", *Waijiao Pinglun*, No. 1, 2010, p. 14.
29. Zi Zhongyun, "*Weile Minzu de Zuigao Liyi, Weile Renmin de Changyuan Fuzhi*", *Taipingyang Xuebao*, No. 4, 1999, p. 11.
30. Han-yi Shaw, "The Diaoyutai/Senkaku Islands Dispute: Its History and an Analysis of the Ownership Claims of the PRC, ROC and Japan," Occasional Papers/Reprints Series, *Contemporary Asian Studies*, No. 3, 1999, School of Law, University of Maryland.

31. Chen I-hsin, "Why Taiwan Cannot Cooperate with the Mainland to Protect the Diaoyu Islands", *Zhongguo Shibao*, July 27, 2012; Zhu Feng, "A Three-Pronged Strategy to Protect the Diaoyu Islands", *Caijing*, September 09, 2012; Wu Di, "The Diaoyu Islands Crisis and the Strategy of 'Hiding one's Talents and Biding one's Time'", *Lianhe Zaobao*, September 15, 2012; *Editorial*, "Clashing Over the Diaoyu Islands", *Caijing*, September 09, 2012.
32. Erik Beukel, "Popular Nationalism in China and the Sino-Japanese Relationship: The Conflict in the East China Sea; An Introductory Study", by the Danish Institute for International Studies, 2011.
33. Shih-Ding Liu, "China's Popular Nationalism on the Internet. Report on the 2005 anti-Japan Network Struggles," *Inter-Asia Cultural Studies*, Vol. 7, No. 1, 2006, pp. 148-149.
34. Chien-peng Chung, "The Diaoyu/Diaoyutai/Senkaku Islands Dispute: Domestic Politics and the Limits of Diplomacy," *American Asian Review*, Vol. 16, No. 3, Fall 1998, p. 159.
35. "Ishihara Says he will Defy Government Orders, Land on Senkaku Islands," *The Asahi Shimbun*, August 25, 2012.
36. Hitoshi Tanaka, "Politicising the Senkaku Islands a Danger to Regional Stability," *East Asia Forum*, August 19, 2012.
37. "Inside Look: Japan Tried but Failed to Avert Disaster in China Dispute," *The Asahi Shimbun*, September 26, 2012.
38. Yukong Huang, "China's Conflict between Economic and Political Liberalization," *SAIS Review*, Vol. 32, No. 2, Summer/Fall 2012, p. 53.
39. Linda Jakobson and Dean Knox, *New Foreign Policy Actors in China*, SIPRI Policy Paper no. 26, Stockholm International Peace Research Institute, September 2010, pp. 43-46.
40. Richard C Bush III, "China-Japan Security Relations," *Brookings Policy Brief Series*, #177, October 12, 2010, cited in Beukel, n. 32.
41. Ibid.
42. Ibid.
43. Kishore Mahbubani, Dean of the Lee Kuan Yew School of Public Policy, National University of Singapore, "Results Matter: Pragmatism Prevails in Asia," *Global Asia*, Vol. 5, No. 1, Spring 2010, pp. 37-42.

44. Shaw, n. 30.
45. The East China Sea Peace Initiative, announced by the Ma Ying-jeou administration in August 2012, released by the Ministry of Foreign Affairs, Republic of China (Taiwan).
46. "Taiwanese President Ma Ying-jeou's remarks on Air Space Security in the East China Sea", International Conference on "Peace and Security in East Asia" February 26, 2014.
47. Shaw, n. 30.
48. For more details, see "Resolution on the Senkaku/Diaoyu Island Dispute," Submitted to the Special Political and Decolonialization Committee, Sponsor: Australia.
49. Zhongqi Pan, "Sino-Japanese Dispute over the Diaoyu/Senkaku Islands: The Pending Controversy from the Chinese Perspective," *Journal of Chinese Political Science*, Vol. 12, No. 1, 2007.
50. Ye Zicheng, *Inside China's Grand Strategy: The Perspective from the People's Republic*, Translated by Steven I Levine and Gouoli Liu, (New Delhi: KW Publishers Pvt Ltd, 2013), p. 156.
51. Andrew Moravcsik, *Liberal Theories of International Relations: A Primer* (Princeton University, 2010).
52. For a detailed debate on this subject, see John J. Mearsheimer, "The Rise of China will Not Be Peaceful at All," *The Australian*, November 18, 2005; also see, "Rivalry in the Offing," *China Security*, Vol. 4, No. 2, Spring 2008; and see, "China's Unpeaceful Rise," *Current History*, vol. 105, no. 690, April 2006.
53. China amended the Regulations of the People's Liberation Army (PLA) on the Political Work in 2003 to add media, psychological, and legal warfares to the PLA's political work; for more details, see US Department of Defense, *Annual Report to Congress: Military and Security Developments Involving the People's Republic of China*, August 2011, which explains the quoted *warfares* in greater detail.
54. M Taylor Fravel, "International Relations Theory and China's Rise: Assessing China's Potential for Territorial Expansion," *International Studies Review*, No. 12, 2010, pp. 505-532.
55. For more details, see Thucydides, "The History of the Peloponnesian

War" cited in, Kenneth John Atchity and Rosemary McKenna, eds., *The Classical Greek Reader* (Oxford University Press, 1998), pp. 157-163.

56. For more details, see Jayadeva Ranade, "What China Will Do Next in the South China Sea," *Rediff.com News*, July 14, 2016.
57. Srikanth Kondapalli, "What the South China Sea Verdict Means," *Rediff.com News*, July 13, 2016.
58. For more details, see Brahma Chellaney, "China's Challenge to the Law of the Sea," Opinion Page, Project Syndicate, July 13, 2016.

7. Submissions for Policy Consideration and Formulation

1. It should be investigated whether China is seeking to alter the status quo through "grey zone" coercion that neither undermines economic cooperation nor triggers military confrontation. This strategy calls for regional players to protect bilateral and multilateral interests against any such "grey zone" pressure in the East and/or South China Seas and integrate the policy to deal with Senkaku-related contingencies.[1]
2. Any potential declaration of an ADIZ in the future by any nation that threatens to destabilise regional peace and security needs to be met with a coordinated multilateral response.
3. Although regional players including Japan, India, and the US (owing to its regional alliance obligations in Asia) need to ensure building, and furthering, a cooperative relationship with China, it, however, should be one which is based on the foundational premise of being on equal terms, while simultaneously ensuring a credible politico-military deterrent to negate coercion / coercive strategies, and ensure lasting peace, stability and security in Asia and the Pacific.

4. Shedding the cloak of being a reluctant player in its strategic backyard, India and partner nations with similar stakes and regional objectives should proactively engage in terms of presence and capacity in the Indo-Pacific and Indian Ocean Regions – with the Pacific Islands and Indian Ocean bound into a single theatre.
5. There is a need for an enhanced defence posture and presence in the Indo-Pacific, stressing unrestricted freedom of navigation, overflight rights, unimpeded lawful commerce, and upholding the principles of sovereignty and territorial integrity.
6. Realisation of a peaceful, open, equitable, stable, secure and rule-based order in the Indo-Pacific region toward 2025 should be prioritised as a primary regional common.
7. An initiative to leverage defence diplomacy should be launched. This can be achieved by establishing a *Multilateral Maritime Affairs Dialogue* among India, Japan, South Korea, Australia, France, Vietnam, Myanmar, Malaysia, Thailand, Seychelles, Singapore, the Philippines, and the US.
8. The above-mentioned nations should invest in building capabilities in the Indo-Pacific, and coordinate for greater interoperability and develop integrated operations with partners.
9. India's proactive approach in the Indo-Pacific corresponds with the "Act East" policy approach and course. This has been visible with the

dispatch of four warships, including a frontline destroyer and a stealth frigate, on a long overseas deployment to the Indian Ocean and South China Sea in May 2015 to kick off exercises with Singapore, followed by making port calls at Jakarta (Indonesia), Freemantle (Australia), Kuantan (Malaysia), Sattahip (Thailand) and Sihanoukville (Cambodia).

10. Given its 7,500 km coastline, 1,200 islands and 2.4 million sq km EEZ, India's reorientation and demonstration of being a consistent security partner for the region highlights New Delhi's maritime interests and stakes in the larger "Indo-Pacific" – a term that has begun to feature more prominently, especially in the Indo-Japanese 2025 vision.

11. The frequency of the India-US-Japan Malabar trilateral naval exercises should be increased and include efforts to enhance mitigation capacity.

12. The September 2015 inaugural India-US-Japan Trilateral Ministerial Dialogue should identify collaborative methodologies that can strengthen regional connectivity, including between South and Southeast Asia, and bolster maritime security.

13. The inaugural Japan-India-Australia Trilateral Dialogue is a significant initiative and should undertake specific decisions that would augment the security architecture in the Indo-Pacific in future discussions.

14. The Indian invitation to Japan for its permanent participation in the bilateral India-US Malabar naval exercises (the first such manoeuvre being in October 2015) needs to be made a regular feature.

15. Indo-Japanese interoperability can be further improved in the emerging maritime expeditionary forces and Air Forces. For this type of cooperation, the US, through its Marine Corps and multinational Red Flag air exercises, can play the potential role of a facilitator.

16. The first ever India-Australia joint naval drill including anti-submarine warfare and coordinated anti-submarine drills held in the Bay of Bengal in September 2015 became a lucid manifestation of India's growing maritime thrust towards the Indo-Pacific, and needs to continue regularly.

17. The June 2016 India, Japan and US annual Malabar naval exercise is the 20th edition of the exercise, and the first after the formal expansion of the bilateral exercise to a trilateral format in 2015. The harbour phase was conducted at Sasebo, and the sea phase took off from the Okinawa prefecture in the Philippine Sea.

18. This naval trilateral should increase interoperability in future manoeuvres among the Indo-Japanese-American Navies and develop closer collaboration for maritime security operations. The major emphasis needs to be on anti-submarine drills

and protection of aircraft carriers from hostile underwater assets.

19. Strengthening of regional security institutions and, as part of this endeavour, the East Asia Summit (EAS) dialogue on political and security issues needs to be reinforced. It should guarantee that the ASEAN forum remains the core of the EAS in so far as multilateral discussions on regional peace and the security agenda in the Indo-Pacific are concerned.

20. Engagement with regional institutions, particularly the ASEAN Defence Ministers Meeting Plus (ADMM-Plus) Experts Working Group (EWG) on Maritime Security remains vital, which seeks to facilitate information-sharing.

21. More focus on an expanded ASEAN Maritime Forum, the Indian Ocean Naval Symposium, and the Western Pacific Naval Symposium; for example, the US PACOM Amphibious Leaders Symposium (PALS) that brought together 23 Pacific partner nations to collaborate on regional amphibious capability development and the cooperative use of amphibious forces.

22. A very vital facet, which seems to go unnoticed, is that France has territories that are geographically and politically close to Asia, and nearly 85 per cent of France's EEZ lies in the Indian and Pacific Oceans. Since the beginning of 2016, the French Navy (until June 2016) deployed three times through the South China Sea.

23. In this backdrop, France, which terms India as its "main strategic partner in Asia since 1997" should be coopted for an expanded joint presence in operational maritime theatres in the region.
24. India should initiate and take the lead to establish a France-India-Japan-Australia Quad Dialogue that undertakes collective responsibility to reinforce security in the region. India's connection with the South Pacific Islands has traditionally been fairly limited, but now seems to be gaining momentum. While France and Australia are ushering in a new phase in their strategic relationship, by virtue of being close collaborators in the South Pacific, it is time for India to coopt in this group vis-a-vis the South Pacific Islands, since nothing is institutionalised or regular about defence cooperation among France, Japan, Australia and India as a quadrilateral group.
25. Moreover, defence cooperation should be amongst the top priorities for bilateral cooperation under the India-Japan Special Strategic and Global Partnership.
26. India and Japan are required to expedite engagement on Defence Exchange and Technology Cooperation (joint research, development and production) and work together to share Security Measures for the Protection of Classified Military Information.

27. Joint Indo-Japanese R&D efforts, particularly focussing on the US-2 amphibian aircraft.
28. India's "Act East" policy and Japan's "Partnership for Quality Infrastructure" remain in sync with each other. Resilient infrastructure that augments connectivity within India, and regionally, is the need of the hour.
29. In the above reference, the role played by Japan's Official Development Assistance (ODA) is critical, given that India remains one of the largest recipients of Japanese ODA. The total commitment of Japanese ODA loans to India in FY 2015 alone reached around 400 billion yen – the highest ever provided to India.
30. India should encourage faster processing of Japanese ODA loans for the improvement of road and rail network connectivity, most critically in India's northeast and the Andaman and Nicobar Islands. India is required to encourage and hold advanced discussions with the Japanese to invest more in infrastructure development all across the northeast region, including in the Indian state of Arunachal Pradesh.
31. The Indian Navy (IN) and Japan Maritime Self-Defence Force (JMSDF) should increasingly coopt and participate in International Fleet Reviews.
32. The Government of Japan and local Okinawa government need to develop and accelerate "quick win" land returns, such as to the Naha port, the

centrepiece of plans for Okinawa's economic rejuvenation. In addition, radar, and missile battery presence on Okinawa, with greater joint use and access to bases, to improve interoperability should be expedited.[2]

33. Acceleration of the relocation of US forces on Okinawa: in the short-term, the Futenma Replacement Facility plan must be completed on schedule. Consideration of relocation of almost half of the 22,000 Marines currently stationed in Okinawa and scheduled to be transferred to Guam, Australia, and Hawaii. This proposal should be accelerated from the current completion date of the early 2030s through earlier construction of facilities in their new locations.[3]

Notes

1. In 2013, the Sasakawa Peace Foundation and the Center for Strategic and International Studies established the Commission on the Future of the Alliance, a bilateral commission co-chaired by Richard Armitage, John Hamre, and Ryozo Kato. The quoted references are some of the *Recommendations for the US-Japan Alliance – A Coordinated China Strategy*, in the "The US-Japan Alliance to 2030: Power and Principle", available at http://spfusa.org/research/the-us-japan-alliance-to-2030-power-and-principle/
2. Ibid.
3. Ibid.

Author's Profile

Dr. Monika Chansoria is a Senior Fellow at the Centre for Land Warfare Studies (CLAWS), New Delhi, where she heads the China-study programme. She holds a Ph.D. in International Relations from the School of International Studies, Jawaharlal Nehru University (JNU), New Delhi, and subsequently, was a recipient of the prestigious French Hérmes Post-Doctoral Fondation Maison des sciences de l'homme Fellowship in Paris.

Dr. Chansoria has been awarded many prominent international academic fellowships, including at the Cooperative Monitoring Centre (Sandia Laboratories, US), Japanese Global Chair of Excellence (Hokkaido University, Sapporo), and the FMSH Senior Fellowship as Visiting Professor and Associate Director of Studies in Paris.

Her list of published work is fairly exhaustive, with authored books, including the present one, being *Nuclear China: A Veiled Secret* (2014), *China: Military Modernisation and Strategy* (2011), and *Chinese WMD Proliferation in Asia: US Response* (2009). Besides, she has co-edited *Pakistan's Tactical Nuclear Weapons: Conflict Redux* (2014).

Dr. Chansoria has contributed several research papers and articles in various edited book volumes, academic journals, and national and international dailies. She is a participant in the Track 1.5 and 2 diplomatic dialogues, and writes a regular column on foreign policy and strategic affairs for *The Sunday Guardian* newspaper.

Index